THE BEST OF CANBERRA

THE BEST OF
Canberra

NEW
HOLLAND

Contents

Welcome to the Australian Capital Territory   14

Welcome to Canberra   18
The People of Canberra   20
Canberra's Personality   22
What Canberra Has That Other Places Don't Have   23

Getting Around   24
Public Transport   26
Going Your Own Way   28
Tourist Information Office   29

The Smart Way to Visit Canberra   30
The Canberra Culture Loop   31

The Government and the Capital   32
Australian Parliament House   34
Australian Government House   36
National Capital Exhibition   39
Museum of Australian Democracy at Old Parliament House   40

War and Remembrance   42
Australian War Memorial   44
Anzac Parade Walk   47

High Art   **48**

National Gallery of Australia   50
National Portrait Gallery   52
Canberra Museum and Gallery   54
Canberra Glassworks   56
Canberra Contemporary Art Space   58
Drill Hall Gallery   60

Museums and Other Cultural Institutions   **62**

National Museum of Australia   64
Australian Institute of Aboriginal and
   Torres Strait Islander Studies   67
National Library of Australia   68
National Film and Sound Archive of Australia   71
High Court of Australia   72

Fun with the Kids   **74**

Canberra Carousel Merry-go-round   76
Questacon   78
CSIRO Discovery Centre at Black Mountain   80
Gold Creek Village   82
National Dinosaur Museum   83
Cockington Green Gardens   84
Ginninderra Village   86

Canberra Walk-In Aviary   87
Canberra Reptile Zoo   87
National Zoo and Aquarium   88
Royal Australian Mint   90
National Arboretum and Pod Playground   93
Boundless – Centenary of Canberra National Playground   94
Australian Institute of Sport and AIS Aquatic Centre   97

On Really Hot Days   **98**
Manuka Swimming Pool   100
Dickson Aquatic Centre   101
Big Splash Waterpark   101
Canberra International Sports & Aquatic Centre   102

Fun if You Have the Time   **106**
Telstra Tower   108
Casino Canberra   110
Chinatown   110
Old Bus Depot Markets   111

The Great Outdoors

The Great Outdoors   **112**

Australian National Botanic Gardens   115
The Gardens around Old Parliament House Tours   116
Lake Burley Griffin   118
Lake Burley Griffin Bike Circuit   119
More on the shores of Lake Burley Griffin   120
Rent a GoBoat   120
Seg Glide Ride   120
MV Southern Cross   121
Balloon Flights   122
Balloon Aloft Canberra   122
Dawn Drifters   123
Floriade – The Annual Outdoor Garden Experience   124

Eateries and Drinkeries   **128**

Fine Dining   128
Bruncheries and Cafes   140
Gastropubs   143
Historic Pubs   145
Traditional Pubs   146
Bars   148
Wineries   153
Breweries   156
Wine and Brewery Tours   157

Outside Australian Parliament House

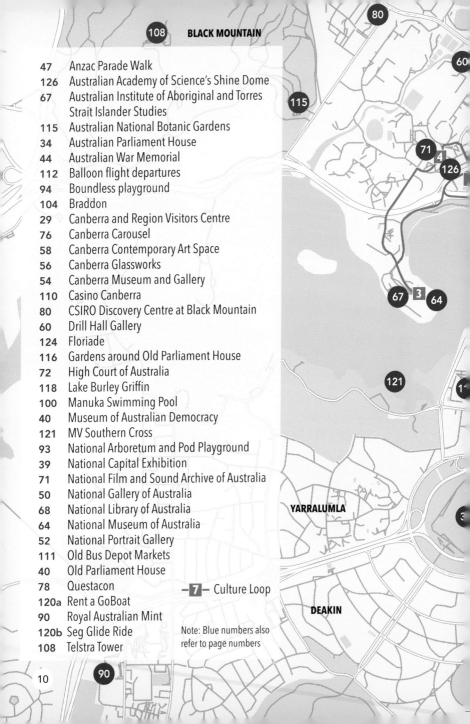

BLACK MOUNTAIN

47	Anzac Parade Walk
126	Australian Academy of Science's Shine Dome
67	Australian Institute of Aboriginal and Torres Strait Islander Studies
115	Australian National Botanic Gardens
34	Australian Parliament House
44	Australian War Memorial
112	Balloon flight departures
94	Boundless playground
104	Braddon
29	Canberra and Region Visitors Centre
76	Canberra Carousel
58	Canberra Contemporary Art Space
56	Canberra Glassworks
54	Canberra Museum and Gallery
110	Casino Canberra
80	CSIRO Discovery Centre at Black Mountain
60	Drill Hall Gallery
124	Floriade
116	Gardens around Old Parliament House
72	High Court of Australia
118	Lake Burley Griffin
100	Manuka Swimming Pool
40	Museum of Australian Democracy
121	MV Southern Cross
93	National Arboretum and Pod Playground
39	National Capital Exhibition
71	National Film and Sound Archive of Australia
50	National Gallery of Australia
68	National Library of Australia
64	National Museum of Australia
52	National Portrait Gallery
111	Old Bus Depot Markets
40	Old Parliament House
78	Questacon
120a	Rent a GoBoat
90	Royal Australian Mint
120b	Seg Glide Ride
108	Telstra Tower

–**7**– Culture Loop

Note: Blue numbers also refer to page numbers

YARRALUMLA

DEAKIN

BRADDON

MOUNT
AINSLIE

CITY
CENTRE

CAMPBELL

Lake Burley Griffin

DUNTROON

MANUKA

KINGSTON

N

11

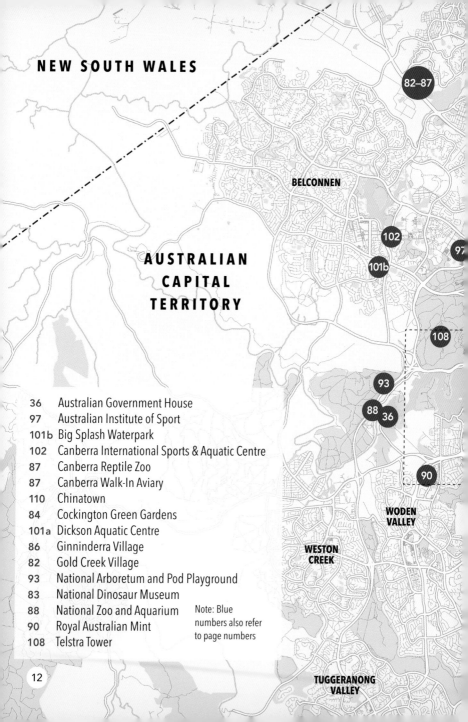

NEW SOUTH WALES

82–87

BELCONNEN

102

97

101b

AUSTRALIAN CAPITAL TERRITORY

108

93

88 **36**

90

WODEN VALLEY

WESTON CREEK

TUGGERANONG VALLEY

36   Australian Government House
97   Australian Institute of Sport
101b Big Splash Waterpark
102 Canberra International Sports & Aquatic Centre
87   Canberra Reptile Zoo
87   Canberra Walk-In Aviary
110 Chinatown
84   Cockington Green Gardens
101a Dickson Aquatic Centre
86   Ginninderra Village
82   Gold Creek Village
93   National Arboretum and Pod Playground
83   National Dinosaur Museum
88   National Zoo and Aquarium
90   Royal Australian Mint
108 Telstra Tower

Note: Blue numbers also refer to page numbers

GUNGAHLIN

NEW SOUTH WALES

NORTH
CANBERRA

110 101a

Mount
Ainslie

(see previous
spread)

SOUTH
CANBERRA

CANBERRA
AIRPORT

FYSHWICK

QUEANBEYAN

N

NEW SOUTH WALES

Welcome to the Australian Capital Territory

Seen on a map, the Australian Capital Territory (the ACT) looks a little like a silhouette of a depressed penguin, staring out to the ocean. Why the odd shape? Apparently, it all has to do with water. But first, a little about why the ACT and Canberra exist in the first place.

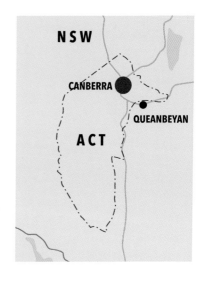

Following the colonial settlement of Sydney by the British in 1788 Australia remained a series of independent colonies, based around what would later become the state capital cities, right through the 1800s. As the decades of the nineteenth century wore on, it became increasingly obvious that Australia was becoming a country in its own right and lobbied with the British parliament for independence. The British basically said, 'Yes, all right' without too much bother and Australia was officially born on 1 January 1901, with its capital in the city of Melbourne.

Why Melbourne? Why not Sydney? Well, that's a long story, but while Sydney and Melbourne contested the point for years prior to independence it seems like Sydneysiders eventually just got tired of arguing and let Melbournians have it. In any case, Australians as a whole came to an arrangement that Melbourne wouldn't be the permanent capital.

Section 125 of the Australian Constitution made provision for the founding of an Australian Capital Territory, which would contain the as-yet-unnamed capital, to be located not closer than 160 kilometers (100 miles) from Sydney, as an enclave within the state of New South Wales. Further provision was also made for another territory, Jervis Bay, to be located due east of the ACT, to allow the capital to have access to the sea.

Why didn't they build the capital on the coast? Because they wanted to develop Australia's vast inland – the same reasoning that created Brasilia in Brazil, but that's another story. Which brings us back to the shape of the ACT.

Australia is the world's driest inhabited continent. Water is important, and it was vital that the capital would have access to adequate supplies of it. It turned out that the Brindabella Range and other nearby mountain ranges together form a neat water catchment area and this area became the line of definition for the ACT. The founding surveyors were confident that a city built in the middle of the catchment area would never lack for water. They were right, and Canberrans remain very proud of their pristine water supply.

So the ACT is basically an amalgamation of water catchment areas. It's 2328 square kilometers (910 square miles) in area, making it just slightly smaller than Luxembourg. New South Wales ceded the land that makes up the ACT to the Commonwealth government in 1911, but because of World War I and other delays, Canberra itself didn't happen immediately.

The ACT is dominated by Canberra and the city takes up the north-east third of the territory. The other two-thirds of the territory is mostly mountainous eucalypt forest: protected areas such as the Buleen Nature Reserve, the Tidbinbilla Nature Reserve and the Namadgi National Park. The climate is oceanic with cool winters, warm to very warm summers and even (but little) rainfall throughout the year.

CIVIC CENTRE

BASIN

BASIN

LAKE

M

GOVERNMENT GROUP

HOUSES of PARLIAMENT

BASIN

Governor General's
Residence

CAPITOL

Welcome
to Canberra

INITIAL CITY

SUBUR

Canberra, Australia's bush capital, had to happen because otherwise Sydney and Melbourne would still be arguing about who would get to be 'it' to this day. In 1911 the Federal Capital Territory – that would later become the ACT – came into existence. In April 1911, the federal government announced an international competition for the design of the capital city, and, in the great tradition of Australian governments giving major architectural commissions to non-Australians, the 1912 prize went to Chicago-based American architect Walter Burley Griffin, who had a life-long collaboration with his wife, Marion Mahony Griffin. Also in the great Australian tradition of bureaucratic interference with the work of visionaries, Griffin ultimately left the project in 1920 but continued to reside in Australia almost until his death in 1937.

Canberra was officially named and established on 12 March 1913. This date is still celebrated as Canberra Day, although with the Australian love of long weekends the holiday is celebrated on the second Monday of March each year.

Although Griffin's initially design wasn't entirely realized because of funding cuts due to World War I and other political compromises, the city we know today is still substantially his vision. It is a planned city of circuits and small suburbs that takes full advantage of its landscape and is very easy to get around in. Whatever squabbles Griffin and the bureaucrats were involved in are now footnotes in history. The architect had always planned to have a central lake in the capital, and in 1964 his wish came true and Lake Burley Griffin was named after him – 'Burley Griffin' because of an ongoing misconception that 'Burley' was part of his surname.

Canberra really is a bush capital. It's surrounded by nature and it has parks and nature reserves coming out of its figurative ears. As Griffin originally envisaged, it's a city unlike any other.

The People of Canberra

The first human inhabitants of the region now occupied by the city of Canberra had been living there for at least 21,000 years and probably longer. Although records are sketchy, the present situation is that there are now four Aboriginal groups contesting traditional ownership of the area. They are: the Ngambri, the Ngambri-Guumaal, the Ngarigo and the Ngunnawal.

Even the name Canberra is subject to differing accounts of its origin. The intention was that it was derived from a Ngunnawal word *kambera* meaning 'meeting place', but one Ngunnawal elder, Don Bell, claims it actually comes from a Ngunnawal word *nganbra* or *nganbira* meaning, respectively, 'woman's breast' and 'hollow between woman's breasts' in reference to the geographical features Mount Ainslie and Black Mountain, and the Sullivan's Creek floodplain that lies between them.

Modern Canberra is a city of almost 400,000 inhabitants, of whom less than 2 per cent are of Aboriginal origin. Around 30 per cent of Canberrans were born overseas and it's a young city, with a median age of 35 and only about 12 per cent of the population over 65. It's also an educated city, with over 40 per cent of the population having an education at least equivalent to a bachelor's degree and the median income is higher than the national average. Like every other Australian, you'll find Canberrans to be a friendly bunch. The most intense arguments you'll get into won't be over sex or religion but over politics, football and cricket.

For decades, the rest of Australia tended to look down upon Canberra as a sort of backwater inhabited by unimaginative politicians and even more unimaginative public servants, but in recent years Canberra has blossomed into a city with a sophisticated population who enjoy intelligent conversation as much as a good football or a cricket game, and good food and wine.

Canberra's Personality

A small proportion of Canberra's population is still made up of an establishment of government workers obsessed with how high they, and you, have climbed up the public service hierarchy (because when they meet you they automatically assume that you're in the public service), but there are also a large number of Canberrans who use a job in Canberra as a stepping stone in a broader career plan. The ACT has the second-highest population turnover of any state or territory in Australia after the Northern Territory.

Having said that though, the general feel of the place is that Canberra has access to everything a reasonable human being could want: safety, stability, culture both high and popular, and access to lovely countryside. Canberra is laid-back. Make friends with this city. There's no reason to hurry here and you'll enjoy it a lot more if you know specifically what you're looking for.

Canberra is relatively small – less than one-tenth the size of Sydney or Melbourne; one-fifth the size of Brisbane or Perth; one-third the size of Adelaide but twice the size of Hobart. The size of Canberra and its clever planning means that everywhere is relatively easy to get to, travel times are relatively short, and you're best off planning your trip to Canberra around your specific interests, which is why this guide book is organized the way it is.

Please Note:
All opening hours of venues are given in AEST (Australian Eastern Standard Time) so you can plan when to call or make bookings just in case you're holding this book in your hot little hand while outside of the ACT/New South Wales time zone.

What Canberra Has That Other Places Don't Have

Australia, for all its vast hinterland, known locally as 'the bush', is predominantly an urban nation, with more than two thirds of its population living in one of the eight capital cities. However, because wild Australia is never far away Australian capital cities are among the least 'urban' cities you're ever likely to see, filled with nature and wildlife, and the least urban of them all is Canberra.

Canberra is a city of parks, gardens and reserves with buildings and roads nestled among them, rather than the other way around. Being the nation's capital, Canberra is the home of major Australian cultural institutions. People come here for the monuments, the history and the culture; especially since there are major artistic exhibitions going on in Canberra all the time.

The public face of Canberra is like the special 'beautiful' room in some people's houses, specifically designed for guests to show off the family photographs and all the nicest things that the family owns. Only in this case, the family is the whole of the Australian nation, and the porcelain that's too good to use and lives in the glass cabinets are memorials, art galleries and exhibits on permanent display.

And when you've had enough of all of that human-made sight-seeing, then the bush is only a stone's throw away. In recent years, the food scene in Canberra has also really lifted its game.

All opening hours, admission prices and other costs are correct at the time of publication but are subject to change without notice so, if in doubt, please telephone the venue or consult their website before committing to your plans and visits.

Getting Around

Getting to Canberra is easy since as it's linked by plane, coach, rail and road to both Sydney and Melbourne, as well as other Australian cities. Once you're there, if you have your own car you'll find that it's very easy to get around and parking isn't all that hard. In many cases, public transport is also easy to access and to use.

Public Transport

Transport Canberra (TC) is the company that oversees public transport. Canberra has no local rail network, so all public transport is by bus or light rail (tram).

Canberra has several public transport hubs, but until you get to know the place better, the most relevant one for the visitor is City Bus Station.

The Light Rail is Canberra's newest public transport option and opened in 2019 along a single line joining the city center (just north of City Bus Station) along 13 stops to the northern suburb of Gungahlin. Services run from 6.00 am to 11.30 pm Sunday to Thursday and to 1.00 am Friday and Saturday.

Canberra's bus services are integrated and pretty comprehensive and allow access to most areas in the Canberra metropolitan area. If you like maps, or even if you enjoy abstract art, a downloadable map of Canberra's bus routes is available at **www.transport.act.gov.au**.

Bus fares can be paid on the buses themselves but the easier way to do it is to use a **MyWay** card. MyWay cards can be purchased in advance, but you'll have to allow seven days for delivery. There are lots of places you can buy a MyWay card in Canberra, see **www.transport.act.gov.au/tickets-and-myway/get-myway**. If you're already in Canberra, then assuming that you're in Civic – the closest thing that Canberra has to a city center – you can buy MyWay cards at the Supa24 convenience store at 2 Mort Street, City. MyWay cards cost $4 for adults and $2.50 for concessions. Once you have your card, you'll need to put some money into it so that you can get travel credit. This is relatively straightforward and the person selling you your MyWay card can recommend how to go about this.

Bus ticket prices depend on whether you're traveling at peak times or off-peak. But to give you a rough idea, an adult peak-time ticket is about $3, off-peak about $2.60 concession peak $1.70 and off-peak free. The good news is that a single bus ticket allows for up to 90 minutes of unlimited travel time. The best news is that your daily charges for bus travel are capped at about $10 per day for adults and $5 for concession. Buses generally run from about 6.00 am to around 10.30 pm.

For more precise details on getting around go to: **www.transport.act.gov.au/getting-around/journey-planner**. Note, the Journey Planner website can be a little temperamental. It's important to fill in the right information, although you do get prompts. To assume all departure points are from Civic enter 'City Bus Station, City, ACT, Australia' in the 'from' field.

For all Transport Canberra enquiries call 131 710 or +61 2 6207 7611 if you're outside of Australia.

Getting out of Canberra to see the rest of the ACT is a little more difficult but made easier by a number of companies that offer special interest tours. Information about tour groups operating in the ACT is available at **www.visitcanberra.com.au/tour-operators**.

Going Your Own Way

If you want to go your own way there are a number of car-rental companies and Canberra also has Uber and other rideshare services available. Canberra is a city with a highly developed infrastructure and services, but you'll still have problems getting a cab on a Friday or Saturday night if you don't book ahead.

Canberra taxi numbers are:

Australia Wide Taxis	131 008
ACT Cabs	02 6280 0077
Canberra Elite Taxis	02 6126 1600
Cabxpress	1300 222 997
Silver Service Canberra	133 100

Many cab companies offer minibus services if you need to book a cab for more than four people. Wheelchair accessible taxis must be booked ahead on 139 287 or at **www.13wats.com.au**.

Canberra likes to promote ridesharing. If it suits you and you want to try it your options are:

Gocatch	www.gocatch.com
Uber Canberra	www.uber.com/en-AU/cities/canberra
Ola	www.olacabs.com.au
Glide	www.glidetaxi.com.au

In Australia, it is considered polite for at least one passenger to sit up front with the driver, unless you're only traveling as a couple. It's part of our tradition of egalitarianism, which we still pay a lot of lip service to.

Tourist Information Office

The hub of visitor information for Canberra is **www.visitcanberra.com.au**. There is also the **Canberra and Region Visitors Centre** at Regatta Point.

Address: Regatta Point, Barrine Drive, Parkes 2600
Phone: 1300 554 114, 02 6205 0044
Website:
  www.visitcanberra.com.au/canberra-and-region-visitors-centre
How to get there: It's about a 30-minute walk due south from
  City Bus Station, or just catch a bus to Commonwealth Park,
  walk across the park and you're there in 10 minutes, or take the
  FREE **Culture Loop shuttle bus** (page 31) to stop 5.
Opening hours: 9.00 am to 5.00 pm Monday to Friday 9.00 am to
  4.00 pm weekends and public holidays.

The Smart Way to Visit Canberra

Every city in Australia has a list of their must-see attractions, and while what is and isn't on a list depends on who you talk to, and how long that list is, there are always a few attractions that should be on everyone's list. But in the case of Canberra, the city is so small that you could argue that everything is a 'must-see', so the clever way to approach a visit to Canberra is to decide what you're interested in first, and plan around that.

Are you interested in history or art? Do you want to explore food and wine? Do you love the great outdoors? Do you want to visit places that the kids will love too? Or do you want it *all*?

This book is arranged around sites and attractions that have a common theme, so that you can plan your trip accordingly.

THE CANBERRA CULTURE LOOP

If you're really pressed for time and you're a bit of a culture vulture, then the best way to get around is to take advantage of Canberra's FREE shuttle bus – the Culture Loop. The whole circuit takes around 45 minutes and you could take a loop around first without getting off to get your bearings. The bus runs daily from 9.00 am to 5.00 pm and departs from the following stops:

Stop 1: **Canberra Centre** – 17 Akuna Street,
         near the Myer department store

Stop 2: **NewActon**

Stop 3: **National Museum of Australia** (page 64)

Stop 4: **National Film and Sound Archive** (page 71)

Stop 5: **Regatta Point** – **National Capital Exhibition** (page 39)
         and **Canberra and Region Visitors Centre** (page 29)

Stop 6: **National Library of Australia** (page 68)
         and **Questacon** (page 78)

Stop 7: **The Museum of Australian Democracy**
         at **Old Parliament House** (page 40)

Stop 8: **Australian Parliament House** (page 34)

Stop 9: The **Canberra Museum and Gallery** (page 54)

You can download the Culture Loop timetable and map from the link at: nca.gov.au/attractions-and-memorials/culture-loop, or see the map on pages 10–11.

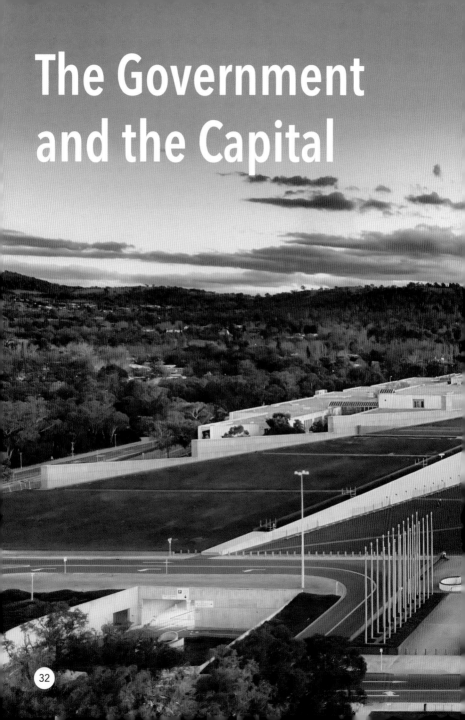

The Government and the Capital

Australian Parliament House

Why you should go: Because it's spectacular, dominates the Canberra skyline and is the seat of Australian democracy. In 1978 the architecture firm of Mitchell, Giurgola and Thorp won the competition for its design out of 329 entries. True to the great Australian tradition, Ehrman Mitchell was American and Romaldo (Aldo) Giurgola was Italian-American; Ric Thorp, at least, is Australian. After ten years work, it opened on 9 May 1988, just a *little* late to be in time for the bicentenary of European colonization. Its 4700 rooms cover some 224,000 square meters (over 2.4 million square feet) on some 13 hectares (32 acres) and 5000 people work there, at least *partly* running the country.

Address: Parliament Drive, Canberra 2600

Phone: 02 6277 7111

Website: **www.aph.gov.au**

How to get there: It's a 10-minute bus ride due south from City Bus Station or take the FREE **Culture Loop shuttle bus** (page 31) to stop 8.

Opening hours: 9.00 am to 5.00 pm seven days, hours extended when parliament is sitting.

Time budget: Several hours.

How much: FREE! But there are also paid tours.

While you're here: Take a free tour. They run five times a day at 9.30 am, 11.00 am, 1.00 pm, 2.00 pm and 3.30 pm and last 40 minutes. Book on the website, by phone or in person at the information desk on the day of your visit. Details of other tours are also available on the website.

Take time to look at the House of Representatives formal gardens, head down the hill to the **Museum of Australian Democracy at Old Parliament House** (page 40), visit one of the other attractions on Lake Burley Griffin such as the **National Gallery of Australia** (page 50), **High Court of Australia** (page 72) or **Questacon** (page 78).

For the Virtual Visitor: You can take a quick peak at **the Lodge,** the official residence of the Prime Minister, which is a short walk south-west at 5 Adelaide Avenue, Deakin. Unfortunately, because it really is a private residence, and a *relatively* small one at that, the Lodge, unlike, say, the White House, isn't usually open to the general public. But you can get a nice idea of what it looks like on the inside by Googling 'Lucy Turnbull's Tour of the Lodge, Canberra' conducted by the wife of the then Prime Minister Malcolm Turnbull in 2016.

Australian Government House

If you want to get close to the pinnacle of government in Australia, you'll have to go beyond parliament in order to rub shoulders with the Queen's representative in Australia, the governor-general. Government House is the governor-general's official residence and this heritage-listed building is set on 54 hectares (133 acres) of prime Canberra real estate with its own mob of kangaroos (kangaroos come in 'mobs' not 'herds'), located on the south-western shores of Lake Burley Griffin, just east of the **National Zoo and Aquarium** (page 88). The bad news is that the house and grounds are usually closed to the general public because it's busy all year round with official ceremonies and hosting school groups. However, there is a nice view of the building from the Government House lookout on Lady Denman Drive at Scrivener Dam.

Address: Dunrossil Drive, Yarralumla 2600

Phone: 02 6283 3533

Website: **www.gg.gov.au**

How to get there: There's no bus service to Government House but if you like walking the number 58 bus will take you as far as Dunstan Street near Murdoch Street in Curtin.

Opening Hours: Generally not open to the public but keep an eye out for open days during the year, usually announced several weeks before they happen (check the website regularly for details).

Time budget: A couple of hours if you're using public transport or walking.

onal Capital Exhibition
Welcome to the
National Capital Exhibition

National Capital Exhibition

Why you should go: The NCE is a permanent exhibition about Canberra and its history. It's a great first stop so that you can get your bearings and it gives you context for everything else you'll see from here.

Address: Barrine Drive, Parkes 2600

Phone: 02 6272 2902

Website: **www.nca.gov.au/nce**

How to get there: Take the FREE **Culture Loop shuttle bus** (page 31) to stop 5, or it's about 30 minutes' walk due south from City Bus Station, or just catch a bus to Commonwealth Park, walk across the park and you're there in 10 minutes.

Opening hours: 9.00 am to 5.00 pm Monday to Friday, 10.00 am to 4.00 pm Saturday and Sunday.

Time budget: One hour.

How much: FREE!

While you're here: You're in the same building as the **Canberra and Region Visitors Centre,** so, having been inspired by what you've seen and heard you can plan your next move.

On a nice day a stroll around Lake Burley Griffin is a lovely way to spend some time. The much photographed **Captain James Cook Memorial globe and water jet** are located right in front of the National Capital Exhibition and Regatta Point. The jet operates from 11.00 am to 2.00 pm daily, subject to weather conditions and maintenance.

Museum of Australian Democracy
Old Parliament House

Why you should go: Before the current Parliament House, Australia had another Parliament House that served the nation between 1927 and 1988. The building officially became the Museum of Australian Democracy at Old Parliament House on 9 May 1988. Its library served as an interim **National Portrait Gallery** until the new building opened in 2009 (page 52). As the name suggests, it's now a 'living museum' dedicated to highlighting Australia's social and political history. It's full of stuff that even a lot of Australians don't know about Australia.

Address: 18 King George Terrace, Parkes 2600

Phone: 02 6270 8222

Website: **www.moadoph.gov.au**

How to get there: It's a 10-minute bus ride due south from City Bus Station or take the FREE **Culture Loop shuttle bus** (page 31) to stop 7.

Opening hours: 9.00 am to 5.00 pm seven days.

Time budget: At least an hour.

How much: Adults $2, concessions and children over 5 $1, children under 5 FREE, families (2 adults and all dependent children) $5.

While you're here: The MOAD has a number of different tours on offer to deepen your experience of the place including the 45-minute highlights tour (FREE after admission) that runs four times a day and last 45 minutes. Insights tours and Indigenous Experiences of Democracy tours are also available (bookings essential, visit the website or call for details). The Top Secret Tour is a special, two-hour tour that starts at 7.30 pm sharp and *only happens twice a year in September*. Tickets often sell out quickly. This is a must if you happen to be in Canberra at the time. Tickets $59 per person (adults over 16).

Take some time to visit the lovely **rose gardens** on either side of Old Parliament House, open 7 am to 8 pm in summer and 7 am to 5 pm in winter (page 116).

You're also a short walk away from all the major attractions along Lake Burley Griffin.

War and Remembrance

Unfortunately, the history of most nations includes the tragedy of war and conflict. Even Australia, one of the most peaceful nations in the world, has had to deal with the complexities of international struggles. Being the national capital, Canberra has more monuments commemorating military conflict than any other Australian city.

Australian War Memorial

Why you should go: The Australian War Memorial is the largest and most comprehensive source of Australia's military history. Part memorial, part museum, part archive, gallery and library, the memorial, housed in an extraordinary Byzantine-style building, describes itself as 'Canberra's most poignant attraction', and it really is. The War Memorial is not in the least a celebration of war, but an institution dedicated to remembering the sacrifices of earlier generations to preserve the Australian way of life.

Address: Treloar Crescent, Campbell 2600

Phone: 02 6243 4211

Website: **www.awm.gov.au**

How to get there: It's a pleasant 30-minute slow stroll due east from City Bus Station. The bus services don't really save you any time since they only take you halfway. If mobility is a real issue, you're better off catching a cab.

Opening hours: 10.00 am to 5.00 pm seven days.

Time budget: Three hours to do the War Memorial minimal justice.

How much: FREE! Including free wheelchair hire if you need it.

While you're here: Although there are permanent exhibits, there are also temporary exhibits, so even if you've visited before, it's likely that every new visit will bring a fresh experience. There are a variety of FREE guided tours every day starting from 10.00 am hosted by volunteers. The tours are 60 to 90 minutes long. Self-guided audio tours are also available for $10. If you time your visit for the end of the day be sure to stay for the moving Last Post ceremony, held just before closing time, which commemorates a different Australian lost in war each day.

Just outside the War Memorial is Anzac Park and the **Anzac Parade Walk** (page 47).

Anzac Parade Walk

Why you should go: The Anzac Parade walk is a commemorative way lined with war memorials just outside and south of the **Australian War Memorial**. When the weather is good, a pleasant, easy stroll becomes a historical experience that adds even more depth to the War Memorial visit. The Anzac Parade walk was completed in 1965, to coincide with the fiftieth anniversary of the ANZAC landing at Gallipoli.

Address: Anzac Parade, Campbell 2600

Website: **www.nca.gov.au/anzac**

How to get there: It's a pleasant half-hour stroll south-east from City Bus Station. The bus services only take 10 minutes, but they leave you at the southern point of walk.

Time budget: 90 minutes to take a leisurely, self-guided tour.

How much: FREE! Download the Anzac Parade Walking Tour flyer from the website.

While You're Here: There are some 65 war memorials dotted throughout Canberra and while most are to be found within a walking distance of the **Australian War Memorial** there are others a little further out. For further information go to **www.placesofpride. awm.gov.au** and enter 'Search By: Location State: ACT' or if you have a specific interest, ask when you're at the Australian War Memorial.

High Art

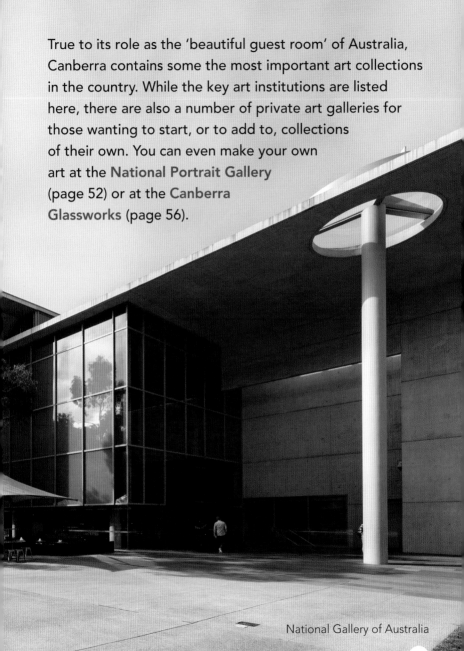

True to its role as the 'beautiful guest room' of Australia, Canberra contains some the most important art collections in the country. While the key art institutions are listed here, there are also a number of private art galleries for those wanting to start, or to add to, collections of their own. You can even make your own art at the National Portrait Gallery (page 52) or at the Canberra Glassworks (page 56).

National Gallery of Australia

49

National Gallery of Australia

Why you should go: This august organization was established as a national public visual art institution. The striking, brutalist-style gallery eventually opened in 1982 after a lengthy and troubled design and construction process. The NGA is one of Australia's largest art museums and its vision is 'to be an inspiration for the people of Australia', and presumably everyone else who visits it too. Highlights include Monet's *Water Lilies*, Pollock's *Blue Poles* and the largest single collection of Aboriginal and Torres Strait Islander art in the world.

Address: Parkes Place, Parkes 2600

Phone: 02 6240 6411

Website: **www.nga.gov.au**

How to get there: It's a 10-minute bus ride due south from City Bus Station or take the FREE **Culture Loop shuttle bus** (page 31) to stop 6.

Opening hours: 10.00 am to 5.00 pm seven days.

Time budget: Three hours minimum. Of course, you could spend days here. How much art can you take?

How much: FREE! Wheelchairs and motorized scooters are also available free if you need them – bookings recommended.

While you're here: FREE NGA highlight tours are available every day at 10.30 am, 11.30 am, 12.30 pm, 1.30 pm and 2.30 pm. Bookings are not essential. Special exhibition tours vary in timing, price and booking requirements. Special access tours are also available, and the staff are most accommodating. Call 02 6240 6502 for enquiries.

Don't miss the large sculptural Skyspace installation *Within Without*, by American artist James Turrell, on the southern side of the gallery. The experience changes with the light and shadows throughout the day.

The **Sculpture Garden** on the northern side of the gallery is also not to be missed. Highlights include the interactive fog sculpture by Japanese artist Fujiko Nakaya, the polished metalic *Cones* by Bert Flugelman and Antony Gormley's *Angel of the North*.

National Portrait Gallery

Why you should go: The NPG is the younger and smaller sibling of the NGA and, as the name implies, it is specifically all about the human face. Its portraiture is not limited to painting but also to photography, sculpture and all sorts of other media. Check the website before visiting as the gallery was due to reopen in late August 2019 after building works.

Address: King Edward Terrace, Parkes 2600

Phone: 02 6102 7000

Website: **www.portrait.gov.au**

How to get there: Take the FREE **Culture Loop shuttle bus** (page 31) to stop 6. The Portrait Gallery is located in front of the **High Court of Australia** and next to the **National Gallery of Australia.**

Opening hours: 10.00 am to 5.00 pm seven days.

Time budget: At least an hour.

How much: FREE! Donations are always gratefully accepted. Daily tours are also FREE. Special exhibitions might incur charges and require bookings.

While you're here: The National Portrait Gallery also runs the occasional tour and even masterclasses. See the website for more details. You're close to all the attractions of the Parliamentary Triangle.

Canberra Museum and Gallery

Why you should go: The Canberra Museum and Gallery is a permanent exhibition space that celebrates the social history and visual arts of the Canberra region, including works by Aboriginal and Torres Strait Islanders, in particular the Ngunnawal people of the region. It is also a venue that has a constant stream of interesting exhibitions, so it's *very* eclectic and a delight to visit if you like variety in your art spaces. The CMAG also houses the **Nolan Foundation Collection** – a must-see if you're a fan of the renowned Australian artist Sidney Nolan. It's also small, so visiting it doesn't require a huge commitment.

Address: Corner of London Circuit and City Square, Canberra City 2600

Phone: 02 6207 3968

Website: **www.cmag.com.au**

How to get there: It's right in the heart of the city. If you're coming from any one of the other attractions on the FREE **Culture Loop shuttle bus** (page 31) it's at the last stop, stop 9. You can also catch the Culture Loop from here to any one of the other attractions on that run.

Opening hours: 10.00 am to 5.00 pm Monday to Saturday.

Time budget: About an hour.

How much: FREE!

While you're here: You're not far from the **Canberra Carousel** (page 76) or the **Canberra Contemporary Art Space** (page 58). You might want to breakfast at the **Blue Olive Cafe** (page 140) before going. There are also many options for food, drinks or coffee in the cool **NewActon** precinct, with its innovative architecture, including **Mocan and Green Grout** (page 141).

Canberra Glassworks

Why you should go: Glass is a fascinating, hugely under-appreciated but highly demanding artistic medium. The Canberra Glassworks, located in the historic **Kingston Power House**, is loads of fun. It's not only an exhibition space but a space for working artists where you can actually watch them in the throes of their creation. It's also interactive and you can make your own pieces there.

Address: 11 Wentworth Avenue, Kingston 2600

Phone: 02 6260 7005

Website: **www.canberraglassworks.com**

How to get there: Take the number 2 bus from City Bus Station to Wentworth Avenue, just after Telopea Park. Check the Transport Canberra Journey Planner for details.

Opening hours: 10.00 am to 4.00 pm Wednesday to Sunday.

Time budget: At least an hour.

How much: FREE! But the classes and workshops they run incur fees and require bookings. In a one-on-one expertly guided teaching session you can make your own paperweight or bird for $80 in 20 minutes or your own tumbler or vase for $120 in 40 minutes! Bookings essential.

While you're here: The ever-popular **Brodburger** burger restaurant is attached to the Glassworks. If you're after something other than great burgers then you're just across the road from the bars and restaurants of **Kingston Foreshore** (page 134). If you're visiting on a Sunday between 10.00 am and 4.00 pm you can wander through the **Old Bus Depot Markets** (page 111) right next door.

Canberra Contemporary Art Space

Why you should go: If your tastes run to small, intimate art galleries and you like contemporary art, the CCAS might work for you. CCAS is a contemporary art space at two locations – Gorman House in Braddon and Manuka – with exhibitions by local, national and international artists.

Address: Gorman Art Centre, Gorman House, 55 Ainslie Avenue, Braddon 2612 and 19 Furneaux Street, Manuka 2603

Phone: 02 6247 0188 (Gorman Art Centre) or 02 6247 0188 (Manuka)

Website: **www.ccas.com.au**

How to get there: The **Gorman Art Centre** is a short walk north-east of Civic; the Manuka gallery is located adjacent to

the Manuka shops and the 56 bus runs between the city and Fyshwick via Manuka.

Hours: 11.00 am to 5.00 pm Tuesday to Saturday (Gorman Art Centre); 11.00 am to 5.00 pm Friday to Sunday (Manuka).

Time budget: Open. We suggest visiting the website first to find out if there's anything that tickles your fancy.

How much: FREE! But donations are always appreciated.

While you're here: If you're at the **Gorman Art Centre** site, explore the interesting shops, bars and restaurants of hipster Braddon. You're a short walk from **Civic**, or the **Australian War Memorial** (page 44). If you're at the Manuka site, take a walk around the Manuka shops and observe the locals, walk a little east and have a meal at the historic **Kingston Hotel** pub (page 146).

Drill Hall Gallery

Why you should go: The Drill Hall Gallery is a small gallery affiliated with the Australian National University. Housed in a lovely 1940s building, the emphasis is on a 'selective program of high-quality exhibitions of Australian and international art'. Australian artist Sidney Nolan's nine-panel *Riverbend* is on permanent display.
Address: Kingsley Street, off Barry Drive, Acton 2601
Phone: 02 6125 5832
Website: **www.dhg.anu.edu.au**

How to get there: It's a 10-minute walk north-west of City Bus Station.

Hours: 10.00 am to 5.00 pm Wednesday to Sunday.

Time budget: Open. We suggest visiting the website or calling them first to find out what's on.

How much: FREE! But donations are always welcome.

While you're here: You're on the grounds of the Australian National University and if you walk north-west for 10 minutes you'll reach the **CSIRO Discovery Centre at Black Mountain** (page 80). You're also not far from the **Australian National Botanic Gardens** (page 115).

Museums and Other Cultural Institutions

Culture isn't just about art, it's about history, knowledge and human achievement, and Canberra is home to some of Australia's major cultural institutions.

National Library of Australia

National Museum of Australia

Why you should go: Because you are going to find over 50,000 years of Australian and world cultural history and heritage, as well of millions of years of natural history inside a spectacular, waterfront building. The museum focuses on Indigenous history and culture, European settlement and the interaction between people and the environment. There are also regular major international exhibitions.

Address: Lawson Crescent, Acton Peninsula 2601

Phone: 02 6208 5000 or 1800 026 132

Website: **www.nma.gov.au**

How to get there: It's a 10-minute bus ride south-west from City Bus Station or take the FREE **Culture Loop shuttle bus** (page 31) to stop 3.

Hours: 9.00 am to 5.00 pm seven days.

Time budget: At least two hours.

How much: FREE! But donations are always welcome. Special exhibitions incur a charge and might require bookings. Free guided tours lasting one hour depart daily at 10.00 am and 1.00 pm. The First Australians tour departs from the information desk daily at 3.00 pm, adults $15, concessions and children (over 5 years) $10, family (2 adults and up to 4 children) $40.

While you're here: You're right next door to the **Australian Institute of Aboriginal and Torres Strait Islander Studies** (page 67).

national museum of australia

Australian Institute of Aboriginal and Torres Strait Islander Studies

Why you should go: If you have a specific interest in learning more about Australian Aboriginal culture, then this is the place to go. It holds the world's largest collection of artifacts and documents dedicated to Aboriginal and Torres Strait Islander cultures and preserves over 6 million feet of film, 700,000 photographs, 35,000 hours of sound and houses rare books and manuscripts dating back to 1818. It's also a center for cultural exchange between indigenous communities worldwide.

Address: 51 Lawson Crescent, Acton Peninsula 2601

Phone: 02 6246 1111

Website: **www.aiatsis.gov.au**

How to get there: Take the FREE **Culture Loop shuttle bus** (page 31) to stop 3.

Hours: 9.00 am to 5.00 pm Monday to Friday.

Time budget: At least an hour.

How much: FREE! But donations are always welcome.

While you're here: You're right next door to the **National Museum of Australia** (page 64).

National Library of Australia

Why you should go: If books and the written word are your thing then this is the place to go. Every book published in Australia is required by law to donate a copy to the NLA, so it's the largest reference library in the country. If it's not here, it's not likely to be anywhere else on the continent. Aside from books it also houses collections of images and printed ephemera and there's always at least one special exhibition on.

Address: Parkes Place West, Parkes 2600

Phone: 02 6262 1111

Website: **www.nla.gov.au**

How to get there: It's a 10-minute bus ride due south from

City Bus Station or take the FREE **Culture Loop shuttle bus** (page 31) to stop 6.

Hours: 10.00 am to 8.00 pm Monday to Saturday, 1.30 pm to 5.00 pm Sunday.

Time budget: At least an hour.

How much: FREE!

While you're here: You're close to all the attractions of the Parliamentary Triangle. Have a look at the interesting art and sculptures of **Reconciliation Place,** located between the National Library and **High Court of Australia** (page 72), that serves as a monument to reconciliation between Australia's Indigenous and non-Indigenous peoples. There are 17 works and a self-guided tour with details of the artworks is available at **www.nca.gov.au/tour/ reconciliation-place-walk**.

National Film and Sound Archive of Australia

Why you should go: An absolute must for cinephiles and media junkies. Over 2.8 million items exploring the totality of the moving image and recorded sound in Australia including everything from film, television and radio programs, to documents and artifacts such as photographs, posters, publicity items, scripts, costumes and other memorabilia and vintage equipment.

Address: McCoy Circuit, Acton 2601

Phone: 02 6248 2000

Website: **www.nfsa.gov.au**

How to get there: It's a five-minute bus ride south-west from City Bus Station or take the FREE **Culture Loop shuttle bus** (page 31) to stop 4.

Hours: 10.00 am to 4.00 pm seven days.

Time budget: At least an hour, longer if you're really engaged or if there's a special exhibition on.

How much: FREE! But special exhibitions are either free or very reasonably priced.

While you're here: Continue to ride the **Culture Loop** to the next attraction of your choice. The **NewActon precinct, Parlour** (page 151) and **Monster Kitchen and Bar** (page 133) are a short walk south-east. If you're interested in unusual architecture across the road is the **Shine Dome** of the **Australian Academy of Science** (photo on pages 126–127). If you're lucky, you can see the inside during one of their lectures or on one of their rare open days: **www.science.org.au**

For the virtual visitor, the NFSA collection lends itself beautifully to online experiences and the curators of the institution are not backwards in coming forward: **www.nfsa.gov.au/collection/online-exhibitions**

High Court of Australia

Why you should go: Although you wouldn't think that a courthouse would be a place to go on a holiday the High Court of Australia is actually one of Canberra's major tourist attractions, offering visitors the treat of watching legal proceedings play out with real, live cases, as it's part of the democratic process that courts be open to public scrutiny.

Address: Parkes Place, Parkes 2601

Phone: 02 6270 6811

Website: **www.nla.gov.au**

How to get there: Take the FREE **Culture Loop shuttle bus** (page 31) to stop 6, the High Court is a large box of brutalist concrete and glass. You can't miss it.

Hours: 9: 45 am to 4.30 pm Monday to Saturday. Normal court sitting hours are 10.15 am to 12.45 pm and 2.15 pm to 4.15 pm. We recommend phoning first if you want to enquire about talks by court guides. Please also note that this is a real, working court and visitors are required to comply with conditions of entry and abide by court etiquette: **www.hcourt.gov.au/about/court-etiquette**.

Time budget: At least an hour.

How much: FREE!

While you're here: You're close to a number of other attractions, in order of proximity: the **National Portrait Gallery** (page 52), the **National Gallery of Australia** (page 50), **Questacon** (page 78), the **National Library of Australia** (page 68) and the **Museum of Australian Democracy at Old Parliament House** (page 40).

Fun with the Kids

Some attractions are more child-friendly that others while others are specifically designed to appeal to the under 18s, especially if your kids are really young. Here are some places to visit that you can bring the whole family to that have gone that extra mile to keep the kiddies entertained.

Canberra Carousel Merry-go-round

Why you should go: Because if you're with young kids, or if you're young at heart, this is a small slice of nostalgia that you can indulge in.

Address: 32 Petrie Plaza, Canberra 2601

How to get there: It's right in the heart of the city, a five-minute stroll south-east of the City Bus Station.

Hours: 11.30 am to 2.30 pm Monday to Thursday, 10.30 am to 4 pm Friday, 11.00 am to 3.00 pm Saturday, 10.00 am to 3.00 pm Sunday. Slightly longer hours during daylight savings in the summer.

Time budget: Ten minutes.

How much: $3 per person for a four-minute ride.

While you're here: You're in the center of Canberra, so the whole city is your oyster.

3INFUN CANBERRA TICKET PACKAGE

Canberra is a city of families, so it's no surprise that they've worked out a deal for families for three of the top child-friendly and child-popular attractions. With a **3infun Canberra** ticket you can visit:

Australian Institute of Sport (page 97)
Cockington Green Gardens (page 84)
Questacon (page 78)

If you book online, the packages costs:

Adults $46.50, children, $29.90, seniors $34.20, families (2 adults and up to 3 children) $131.20.

For further information or to purchase **3inFun tickets** online go to: **www.3infun.com.au/tickets**.

Questacon

Why you should go: **Questacon** is the National Science and Technology Centre's showpiece interactive museum designed to 'promote greater understanding and awareness of science and technology within the community'. Like the calmer and more sedate **CSIRO Discovery Centre at Black Mountain** (page 80), it's a total must-visit for science and technology nerds. Even people who aren't usually interested in science love it. It's like a science circus.

Address: King Edward Terrace, Parkes 2600

Phone: 02 6270 2800

Website: **www.questacon.edu.au**

How to get there: It's a 10-minute bus ride due south from City Bus Station or take the FREE **Culture Loop shuttle bus** (page 31) to stop 6.

Hours: 9.00 am to 4.30 pm seven days.

Time budget: At least two hours, but the place is designed to be unashamedly seductive to science buffs and to be fun and engaging. There are shows and activities in the morning and in the afternoon. The ticket is valid for all-day in-and-out entry, so it's not unknown for visitors to spend the entire day at **Questacon** and feel that they've had an amazing day.

How much: Adults $23, children (under 16 years), seniors and students $17.50, families (2 adults and up to 3 children) $70, children under 4 FREE! Note that you can save a lot with a **3infun Ticket** (page 76) if you're interested in visiting the other attractions.

While you're here: Have a look at the interesting art and sculptures of **Reconciliation Place,** located between the **National Library of Australia** (page 68) and the **High Court of Australia** (page 72).

CSIRO Discovery Centre at Black Mountain

Why you should go: The Commonwealth Scientific and Industrial Research Organisation has existed in various incarnations since 1916. Its business is coming up with clever stuff like the components of wi-fi technology, Aerogard insect repellent, introducing the myxomatosis virus to control the pest rabbit population and the development of the polymer banknote. The Discovery Centre offers an interactive journey through CSIRO and Australian science history – a total must-visit for science nerds who want a more reflective and relaxed time than they'll find at **Questacon** (page 78).

Address: North Science Road, Acton 2601

Phone: 02 6246 4646

Website: **www.csiro.au/en/Education/Community-engagement/ Discovery-Centre**

How to get there: From City Bus Station, take the number 32 bus to Barry Drive, almost to the corner of Clunies Ross Street. From there, it's a five-minute walk west.

Hours: 9.00 am to 4.30 pm Monday to Friday.

Time budget: At least an hour, longer if you're really engaged

How much: Adults (over 16 years) $10, seniors and students $7, families (2 adults and up to 3 children) $30.

While you're here: The nearest other attractions are a good 15 minutes' walk to the south-east, but it's a pleasant walk through the grounds of the Australian National University to the **ANU School of Art and Design Gallery** and then further south to the **National Film and Sound Archive** (page 71).

Gold Creek Village

The **Canberra Reptile Zoo** (page 87), **Canberra Walk-In Aviary** (page 87), **Cockington Green Gardens** (page 84), **Ginninderra Village** (page 86), the **George Harcourt Inn** (page 147) and the **National Dinosaur Museum** (page 83) are all within a short walk of each other in Gold Creek Village in the north-western suburb of Nicholls. If you don't have a car then it's a journey that's 1 hour and 15 minutes long by bus *each way*, so if you're going this far you might as well visit all of them and make a day of it.

As getting there by public transport is quite complicated and requires a change of bus, we'd recommend using the Transport Canberra Journey Planner (**www.transport.act.gov.au/getting-around/journey-planner**). A simpler option might be to just catch a cab or Uber – about 25 minutes and $50.

If you're going to go the whole shebang, we recommend the following visiting order: The **National Dinosaur Museum** – **Cockington Green Gardens** – **Ginninderra Village**. By now you'll be hungry for lunch and if you like a traditional pub meal then go to the **George Harcourt Inn**. Now, refueled, you can tackle the **Canberra Walk-In Aviary** and the **Canberra Reptile Zoo**, with optional visits to the **Aboriginal Dreamings Gallery**, the **Aawun Gallery** and **Federation Square**, where there's sure to be somewhere else to eat before you go back to the city.

National Dinosaur Museum

Why you should go: Because it has the largest permanent display of dinosaur and other fossils in the country including some cool life-size models.

Address: 6 Gold Creek Road, Nicholls 2913

Phone: 02 6230 2655

Website: **www.nationaldinosaurmuseum.com.au**

Hours: 10.00 am to 5.00 pm seven days, last admissions at 4.00 pm.

Time budget: At least an hour, longer if you're really engaged.

How much: Adults $16, children under 16 $10.50, seniors and students $12, families (2 adults and 2 children) $45, each extra child $5. FREE public tours are available on weekends and also during the week if you happen to visit during the ACT school holidays.

Cockington Green Gardens

Why you should go: Because it's completely different to the big national museums and monuments of Canberra. Cockington Green is a park filled with handcrafted, miniature buildings from around the world. There's also a miniature train ride. It's like visiting Lilliput. There are also free gas-fired BBQs if you want to bring your own food.

Address: 11 Gold Creek Road, Nicholls 2913

Phone: 02 6230 2272

Website: **www.cockingtongreen.com.au**

Hours: 9.30 am to 5.00 pm seven days, last admissions at 4.15 pm.

Time budget: At least 90 minutes.

How much: Adults $21, children (under 16) $12.50, seniors $15.50, families $59 (2 adults and up to 3 children), each extra child $5. Other deals are available on the website. See also the **3infun Ticket** (page 76).

Ginninderra Village

Why you should go: Ginninderra is not so much a single thing as a collection of buildings and quaint and quirky shops that are a reminder of Canberra's past. The village was built in 1883 and the original schoolhouse and church remain.

Address: O'Hanlon Place, Nicholls 2913

Hours: Approximately 9.00 am to 5.00 pm seven days.

Time budget: Open.

How much: FREE!

Canberra Walk-In Aviary

Why you should go: There are 500 birds representing 60 species and it's your chance to see the descendants of the dinosaurs in a sheltered space.

Address: 18 O'Hanlon Place, Nicholls 2913

Phone: 02 6230 2044

Website: **www.canberrawalkinaviary.com.au**

Hours: May to August 10.00 am to 4.00 pm seven days weather permitting, last entry at 3.30 pm; September to April 10.00 am to 5.00 pm seven days weather permitting, last entry at 4.30 pm.

Time budget: About an hour.

How much: Adults, $15 children (under 16) $10, concessions $13, families $45 (2 adults and 2 children or one adult and three children), each extra child $5, children under 4 free.

Canberra Reptile Zoo

Why you should go: To get up close and personal with the more than 50 species of reptiles and frogs on display.

Address: O'Hanlon Place, Nicholls 2913

Phone: 02 6253 8533

Website: **www.reptilesinc.com.au**

Hours: 10.00 am to 5.00 pm seven days.

Time budget: About an hour.

How much: Adults $16, children (under 16) $10, concessions $11, families (2 adults and 2 children or 1 adult and 3 children) $45, children under 4 free.

National Zoo and Aquarium

Why you should go: Because it's a zoo! And an aquarium! Two attractions in one! What more reason do you need? Highlights include the rare white lions, meerkats, dingoes and the River Systems of the World exhibit.

Address: 99 Lady Denman Drive, Yarralumla 2611

Phone: 02 6287 8400

Website: **www.nationalzoo.com.au**

How to get there: In its infinite wisdom, Transport Canberra decided to discontinue the bus route to the zoo, so there is no longer a public transport option and you will need to drive or catch a taxi or Uber.

Hours: 9.30 am to 5.00 pm seven days.

Time budget: Three hours.

How much: Adults $47, seniors and students $40, children (3 to 15) $26, and families $130 (2 adults and up to 3 children). Carers with ID and Companion Card holders receive free entry with one client.

While you're here: The zoo provides a host of 'close encounters' special zoo experiences to make it an interactive experience with animals like no other. Refer to the website for further information. Entry to the zoo is included in the price of these experiences but you have to book ahead, and special conditions apply. For the truly committed there is the seven-hour **Walk on the Wildside Experience** and you can also stay overnight or longer with a package at the **Jamala Wildlife Lodge** (phone: 02 6287 8444; website: **www.jamalawildlifelodge.com.au**). You're also a 30-minute walk (or a 10-minute cab ride) to the **National Arboretum** (page 93).

Royal Australian Mint

Why you should go: It's where all the coins are made – over 15 billion since 1965. It's a little out of the way but it's *the* place to go to get your numismatic fix.

Address: Denison Street, Deakin 2600

Phone: 02 6202 6999

Website: **www.ramint.gov.au**

How to get there: From City Bus Station take the number 58 bus to Denison Street, near Strickland Crescent. From there it's five-minute walk north-west.

Hours: 8.30 am to 5.00 pm Monday to Friday, 10.00 am to 4.00pn weekends.

Time budget: At least an hour.

How much: FREE!

While you're here: There really isn't anything else nearby, so you might as well head back to town.

National Arboretum Canberra and Pod Playground

Why you should go: Officially opened in 2013, the arboretum is located on the site of pine forests destroyed during the devastating Canberra bushfire of 2003. It features 94 forests of rare, endangered and symbolic trees (most of them still young) from around Australia and the world on a 250 hectare site, and includes the National Bonsai and Penjing collection. There are also striking outdoor sculptures to explore and stunning views across the bush capital. The fabulous nature-themed **Pod Playground** has become one of the most photographed sites in Canberra with its acorn cubbies on stilts and banksia-shaped pods. It offers kids of all ages plenty of challenging opportunities to climb and explore.

Address: 1 Forest Drive, Molonglo Valley, Weston Creek 2611

Phone: 02 6207 8484

Website: **www.nationalarboretum.act.gov.au**

How to get there: Sadly, public transport no longer runs to the arboretum so you will need to drive or take a taxi or Uber.

Hours: Arboretum grounds and Pod Playground open 6 am to 8.30 pm seven days during the warmer months and 7.00 am to 5.30 pm seven days in the cooler months.

Time budget: Open but allow several hours.

How much: FREE! But you will need to pay for parking (to a maximum of $7.80 per day).

While you're here: The **Village Centre** at the heart of the Arboretum features spectacular views and architecture and you can refuel at **Sprout Cafe** or **The Conservatory Restaurant**, or purchase an interesting range of gifts at the shop. You can also bring a picnic and there are plenty of lovely spots to stop and eat.

Boundless – Centenary of Canberra National Playground

Why you should go: Located on the shores of Lake Burley Griffin at Kings Park, it's a place especially younger kids will enjoy frolicking in. It's an all-abilities playground too, so there's something here for everyone.

Address: Kings Park, Wendouree Drive, Parkes 2600

Phone: 02 6207 1075

Website: **www.boundlesscanberra.org.au**

How to get there: Take the FREE **Culture Loop shuttle bus** to stop 5 and it's a lovely lakeside walk of about 20 minutes through Commonwealth Park. Alternatively, it's a 15-minute bus ride (check the Transport Canberra Journey Planner for details) south-east from City Bus Station to the Australian-American Memorial and then a 10-minute walk east.

Hours: 8.00 am to 8.00 pm seven days.

Time budget: Open.

How much: FREE!

While you're here: The historic **Blundells Cottage**, a stone workers cottage built around 1860 (only open Saturdays from 10.00 am to 2.00 pm), is just a short walk west around Lake Burley Griffin. The striking **National Carillon** (an iconic bell tower) is located across a footbridge on Aspen Island and was a gift from the British Government to celebrate the 50th anniversary of the national capital. Listen to recitals on Wednesdays and Sundays from 12.30 pm to 1.20 pm.

Australian Institute of Sport and AIS Aquatic Centre

Why you should go: Because it's the center for Australian high-performance sport and where elite athletes spend a lot of time training to get medals and accolades. It's also the principle research body for sports physiology and medicine and the location of major sports and entertainment events in Canberra (at the adjacent **GIO Stadium** and the **AIS Arena**).

Address: Leverrier Street, Bruce 2617

Phone: 02 6214 1111

Website: **www.experienceais.com**

How to get there: From City Bus Station take the Number 4 bus to College Street, Bruce. Cross the road and catch the Number 9 bus that will take you into the heart of the sports precinct. The trip takes about 40 minutes each way.

Hours: 8.30 am to 5.00 pm Monday to Friday, 9.30 am to 4.00 pm weekends.

Time budget: About three hours, including travel time.

How much: Admission is by paid tour of 90 minutes. Tours run at 10.00 am, 11.30 am, 1.00 pm and 2.30 pm daily; adults $20, children (5 to 17 years) $12, seniors and students $15, families (2 adults and up to 3 children) $55, children under 4 free. However, you can save a lot with a **3infun Ticket** (page 76).

While you're here: Go for a swim at the **AIS Aquatic Centre** which is open from 6.15 am to 9.50 pm Monday to Friday and to 7.50 pm on weekends; adults $6.80, children and concessions $5.20, family swim pass $19.

On Really Hot Days

In the summer months it can, from time to time, get *really* hot in Canberra, so here are a few options if you'd like to take the kiddies (or even just yourself) swimming.

Manuka Swimming Pool

One of Canberra's oldest pools with lovely Art Deco buildings, this outdoor pool is open from October to March. Check the website or call for details. There are a number of buses that travel from Civic to Manuka so check the Transport Canberra Journey Planner for details.
Address: Manuka Circuit, Manuka 2603
Phone: 02 6295 1910
Website: **www.manukapool.com.au**

Dickson Aquatic Centre

Just a short trip from the city center via the new light rail (get off at the Dickson stop), with pools and barbecue areas set amongst trees and lawns. Pool open from October to March, check the website or call for details.

Address: 52 Cowper Street, Dickson 2602

Phone: 02 6247 2972

Website: **www.dicksonaquatic.com.au**

While you're there: You might like to eat at **The Ducks Nuts** (page 144) or one of the many Asian restaurants of Canberra's **Chinatown** (page 110).

Big Splash Waterpark

It's only open in high summer from mid-November to mid-March and it's out in the northern suburbs but if you really want the waterpark experience in Canberra this is the place to go.

Address: 1 Catchpole Street, Macquarie 2614

Phone: 02 6251 1144

Website: **www.bigsplashwaterpark.com.au**

How to get there: Your best option is from City Bus Station to take the Number 32 bus to Bowman Street, Macquarie and then it's just a 5-minute walk north. The trip takes about 35 minutes.

While you're there: Pop into **Ricardo's Cafe** at Jamison Plaza (page 142) and try one of their spectacular cakes.

Canberra International Sports & Aquatic Centre

A year-round place to go swimming (and it has a waterslide!) with a lot of other health facilities if you feel the need to expend extra energy.

Address: 100 Eastern Valley Way, Bruce 2617

Phone: 02 6251 7888

Website: **www.cisac.com.au**

How to get there: From City Bus Station take the Number 4 bus to College Street, Bruce near Eastern Valley Way and you're there. The trip takes about 30 minutes.

Braddon

Just a short walk north of the center of the city, Braddon was once a light industrial area that was home to car dealers and outdoor equipment stores but is now the heart of hipster Canberra and a mecca for the city's creative types. In just a few blocks you'll find dozens of quirky shops, bars, restaurants, cafes and bakeries. The heart of Braddon is Lonsdale Street, between Cooyong Street and Ghiraween Street. In the architectural Ori building at 30 Lonsdale Street you'll find design and fashions stores and cafes including

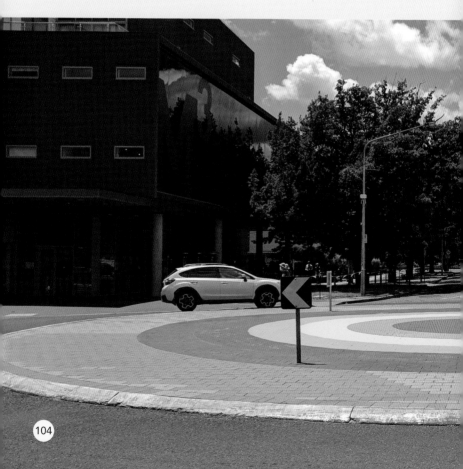

HandsomePretty, **Assemblage Project, Enigma Fine Chocolates,** the florist **Moxom and Whitney** and **Frugii Dessert Laboratory.** Nearby is Canberra's acclaimed homewares store **Bison** (Shop G14, 27 Lonsdale Street) with its tactile ceramics in a range of lovely colors. There are many places to stop if you're hungry, thirsty or in need of caffeine including **Black Fire, Eightysix, Italian and Sons, Lazy Su, Les Bistronomes, Debacle, Hopscotch, The Elk & Pea, The Civic, Bacaro Wine Bar** and **Bentspoke Brewing Company** (see food and drink section (pages 128–157).

Fun if You Have the Time

If you're staying longer in Canberra than you originally planned, or if you've been before and want to experience things just ever so slightly off the beaten tourist path here are a few things you might like to try.

National Carillon

Telstra Tower

The iconic tower on the summit of Black Mountain is visible from all around Canberra. You can drive, or if you're feeling really energetic walk/ride, up Black Mountain Drive to the top of Black Mountain until you reach the 195-meter (640 feet) tall Telstra Tower, which has observation decks, an exhibition space and a cafe.

Address: Black Mountain Drive, Acton 2601

Phone: 02 6219 6120

Website: **www.telstratower.com.au**

Hours: Viewing gallery open 9.00 am to 10 pm daily.

How much: Adults $7.50, children (4 to 16) and seniors $3, families (2 adults and 2 children) $17.

Casino Canberra

Why you should go: Because it's not just a gambling venue. It also includes three restaurants you might like to try – **Natural Nine** (page 136), Pop Yum Cha and The Onyx Lounge.

Address: 21 Binara Street, Canberra 2601

Phone: 02 6243 3700

Website: **www.casinocanberra.com.au**

How to get there: It's an easy 10-minute walk east from the City Bus Station.

Hours: 12.00 pm to 4.00 am seven days.

While you're here: You're close to the center of the city, so anything goes, really.

Chinatown

Canberra's Chinatown is small but if you have a hankering for the far east (or since you're in Australia, the far, far north) you can get your China fix by taking the light rail to the Dickson stop. You'll find many Asian restaurants and Asian grocery stores on and around Woolley Street in Dickson.

Old Bus Depot Markets

Located just next to the **Canberra Glassworks** (page 56) and open on Sunday from 10.00 am to 5.00 pm, the markets are a great source of local produce, handmade clothing and crafts and vintage furniture, clothing and collectables. There are also many delicious food stalls.

Address: 21 Wentworth Avenue, Kingston 2604

Website: **www.obdm.com.au**

How to get there: Take the Number 2 bus from City Bus Station to Wentworth Avenue, just after Telopea Park.

The Great Outdoors

Being a city of parks and gardens, not all of Canberra's attractions lie within roofed walls and the city has a lot to offer the outdoorsy adventurer. Canberra is a city that strongly encourages walking and bicycle riding. In fact, there are bike racks on all Transport Canberra buses and light rail. Transport Canberra doesn't even charge you extra for taking your bike on board. They call the initiative Bike and Ride. For more information visit **www.transport.act.gov.au/ about-us/public-transport-options/bike-and-ride**

If you haven't brought your own bike, you can rent one from Share A Bike: shareabike.com.au; phone 1300 588 533.

Your Guide to Cycling in Canberra can be purchased in person for $5 from the Canberra and Region Visitor's Centre at **www.visitcanberra.com.au/ canberra-and-region-visitors-centre** or Pedal Power at **www.pedalpower.org.au.**

For those who have more time or enjoy a physical challenge, Canberra and the ACT have a number of parklands and nature reserves of which the walker/hiker or bicycler can avail themselves. Looking closely on a map, you'll notice that many are clustered together and loosely interconnect.

These trails range in difficulty from easy to challenging depending on your experience and fitness level and you will need to plan these walks/hikes/tours before you attempt them. Of special note is the Centenary Trail – the 145-kilometer (90 mile) hike around the perimeter of the ACT which takes at least three days and is considered a Grade Three Walk (**www.australianhiker.com.au/trails/ canberra-centenary-trail-act-145km**). But let's start easy ...

Australian National Botanic Gardens

Why you should go: Located on the slopes of Black Mountain, the Australian National Botanic Gardens maintains a scientific collection of native plants from all parts of Australia – around a third of Australia's flora is represented – in a bush setting. A must for lovers of Australian flora, the gardens are organized around different themes or regions, and the **Rainforest Gully** is always a highlight.

Address: Clunies Ross Street, Acton 2601

Phone: 02 6250 9588

Website: **www.anbg.gov.au**

How to get there: The public transport to the gardens is hardly worth the effort, so it's a walk or bike ride west from the city center (around 2.5 kilometers/1.5 miles) through the grounds of the Australian National University until you get to Clunies Ross Street, then it's just a short journey uphill. Otherwise, you can drive (there is paid parking on site) or take a taxi or Uber.

Hours: 8.30 am to 5.00 pm seven days.

Time budget: At least three hours, including travel time to and from the city.

How much: FREE! Free one-hour guided walks are available daily at 11 am and 2 pm, meet outside the visitor center.

While you're here: If you're hungry then Pollen cafe and restaurant is open daily. Check the website before you go as the gardens host a range of interesting talks and exhibitions, and there is a Summer Sounds concert series. There's a Bushland Nature Walk just south that you access through Black Mountain Drive. You're not far from the ANU's **Drill Hall gallery** (page 60).

The Gardens around Old Parliament House Tours

Canberra is a city of gardens, and there are a number of lovely ones to explore, including **Lennox Gardens** (incorporating the **Beijing Garden** and **Canberra-Nara Peace Park)**, which is located behind the **Hyatt Hotel Canberra** on Lake Burley Griffin, and the gardens around **Old Parliament House** (page 40). The gardens were planted between 1931 and 1938, with Robert Broinowski, the Secretary of the Joint House Department, driving the establishment of the rose gardens and display beds. When new **Parliament House** (page 34) was opened in 1988 the gardens fell into disrepair before a program to reconstruct and replant the gardens began around 2000.

You could spend an hour or two wandering the gardens if you take time to linger and smell all the roses. One of the best things about these tours is that all the gardens are FREE. The gardens are open from 7.00 am to 8.00 pm in the summer (during daylight savings time) and 7.00 am to 5.00 pm in the winter.

If you want to take a self-guided tour, you have a several alternatives: go to: **www.nca.gov.au/attractions-and-memorials/old-parliament-house-gardens** and see if there are any special tours advertised because of special occasions. If not, download the FREE Old Parliament House Self-Guided Walking Tour from the website. Copies of this self-guided tour are also available at the **Canberra and Regional Visitors Centre** (page 29).

Lake Burley Griffin

When the locals want to take a walk around Lake Burley Griffin they take the short route – the bridge to bridge walk. This 5-kilometer (3 miles) walk takes you on a journey from the **National Capital Exhibition** (page 39) and along the northern shore to the Kings Avenue Bridge, across the water and through the west end of the cultural district, where the **National Gallery of Australia** is (page 50), then hugging the southern shore until you get to the Commonwealth Avenue Bridge, then across the water again and ending up at the Japanese cherry trees, not so far from the **Captain James Cook Memorial globe and water jet** where you first started, more or less. Yes, there are coffee stands dotted along the way if you run out of energy.
Difficulty: Easy

Trip Time: Two hours.

Tour map download: **www.nca.gov.au/lake-burley-griffin-self-guided-walking-tour**

Lake Burley Griffin Bike Circuit

This is a 28 to 35 kilometer (17 to 22 mile) run around the entirety of Lake Burley Griffin, depending on whether or not you hug the coast taking every little peninsula detour or not. Ditto the coffee stands.

Difficulty: Moderate

Trip Time: This takes an experienced rider just over an hour. It's much longer if you're taking your time. Have a look online for maps of the route.

More on the shores of Lake Burley Griffin

The lake has a variety of experiences on offer run by private companies. Some highlights include:

Rent a GoBoat

GoBoats are small, electric powered boats that do not require a boat licence to use. Ideally suited for a family or group of friends (up to eight people per boat) who've packed their own picnic and want to have it on the water.

Where: Wharf 2, Trevillian Quay, Kingston 2604 (near the
   Canberra Glassworks (page 56))
Phone: 02 6100 7776
Website: **www.goboatcanberra.com.au**
When: Daylight hours – weather permitting.
How much: $99 for the first hour, much cheaper after that,
   especially in the off-season. Bookings essential.

Seg Glide Ride

For those of you who have trouble walking, but aren't in a wheelchair, or even if you just want to give your legs a rest and have a bit of fun, you could try a Segway. Seg Glide Ride rents out Segways and you go on a professionally guided tour around the lake. It's professionally guided because riding a Segway requires a

little training. Riders must be over 12 years old and weigh less than 120 kilograms (265 pounds).

Where: Tours leave from West Kiosk, Queen Elizabeth Terrace, – just down the street from **Questacon** (page 78) and almost right in front of the **Water's Edge Restaurant** (page 139).

Phone: 0406 379 518

Website: **www.seggliderride.com.au**

When: Tours depart throughout the day from 9.30 am until 3.30 pm.

How much: $28 for 15 minutes, $45 for 30 minutes, $65 for an hour. Bookings essential.

MV Southern Cross

For those who prefer that someone else does the piloting, there are a number of cruises available from MV *Southern Cross* including daily sightseeing, lunch and dinner cruises.

Where: A variety of wharves around Lake Burley Griffin. Refer to the website or phone ahead to enquire and book.

Phone: 02 6273 1784

Website: **www.mvsoutherncross.com.au**

When: Cruises start as early as 10.00 am departure and as late as 7.30 pm departure and take from 90 minutes to 3 hours.

How much: Prices start from adults $20, children (5 to 12 years) $10, concessions $15. Bookings essential.

Balloon Flights

Hot air balloons floating across the sky are a regular sight in Canberra and the Canberra Balloon Spectacular is an annual event attracting balloons from around Australia and across the world. For those who want to experience Canberra from on high a balloon flight is an unforgettable thrill.

Balloon Aloft Canberra

Where: Meet in the foyer of the Hyatt Hotel,
    Commonwealth Avenue, Yarralumla
Phone: 02 6249 8660
Website: balloonaloftcanberra.com.au
When: Daily, but you need to book at least 24 hours ahead.
    Passengers meet 30 minutes before sunrise to take advantage of
    the brilliant colors of dawn light.
Time budget: Around three hours to allow for pre-meeting,

45 minutes for the flight, and longer if you're having breakfast at the hotel afterwards.

How much: Prices start from adults $330, children (6–12 years) $240 on weekdays, with an additional charge for a full buffet breakfast.

Dawn Drifters

Dawn Drifters offer a very similar experience to Balloon Aloft.

Where: Meet at dawn at the Hyatt Hotel, usually between 5.00 am and 6.30 am, depending on the time of year

Phone: 02 6248 8200

Website: **www.dawndrifters.com.au**

When: Daily, bookings essential and you must call in advance on the day to check the weather conditions are suitable for flying.

How much: Prices start from adults $310, children (6–12 years) $220 on weekdays with an additional charge for a full buffet breakfast.

Floriade – The Annual Outdoor Garden Experience

Floriade is Canberra's celebration of flowers and spring. This massive outdoor display of flowers is an opportunity to see a riot of color and to be seduced by scent. It is to be avoided at all costs by hayfever sufferers but it's a huge thrill for those who love plants. Where: Commonwealth Park. Take the FREE **Culture Loop shuttle bus** to stop 5.

When: Annually from mid-September to mid-October. Open from 9.30 am to 5.30 pm weather permitting.

How much: FREE! But there are a variety of vendors offering activities or from which you can purchase food or souvenirs.

While You're There: There's also **Floriade NightFest** in the second week of October with the displays lit up with a million bulbs and live music. Open from 6.30 pm to 10.30 pm weather permitting.

Australian Academy of Science's Shine Dome

Eateries and Drinkeries

Obviously, after the considerable exertions involved in enjoying your stay in Canberra, you're going to have to eat at some point, and where and on what will depend on your whims, moods and, literally, your tastes.

Naturally, restaurants often change their menus and even their opening times depending on season and time of the year, so we can only offer an approximate idea of highly recommended venues and it's best to check their website for their current status.

Fine Dining

Canberra used to be considered less wonderful than Melbourne or Sydney when it came to eating out, but in recent years the place has really lifted its game. In spite of being a capital city Canberra is still a small town, and if the food or service is rubbish it doesn't take long for the word to spread, so an eatery really has to be on the ball to survive here.

Here is a selection of the finest dining experiences Canberra currently has to offer that have met with the approval of both visitors and locals. Some of them might be a little out of the way but a little distance never deters a true foodie.

Akiba

40 Bunda Street, Canberra 2601

Open: 11.30 am to 12.00 am Sunday to Wednesday 11.30 am to 2.00 am Thursday to Saturday

Phone: 02 6162 0602

Website: **www.akiba.com.au**

Known for: Casual dining with creative, wood-fired Asian BBQ fare and exotic cocktails in a buzzing ambience.

Aubergine

18 Barker Street, Griffith 2603

Open: Dinner from 6.00 pm Monday to Saturday

Phone: 02 6260 8666

Website: **www.aubergine.com.au**

Known for: Acclaimed creative modern Australian fine dining with elegant decor in a suburban location.

Black Fire

45/38 Mort Street, Braddon. 2612

Open: Breakfast 10.00 am to 11:45am weekends, lunch 12.00 pm to 2.30 pm Monday to Sunday, dinner 6.00 pm to late Monday to Sunday

Phone: 02 6230 5921

Website: **www.blackfirecanberra.com.au**

Known for: Spanish Mediterranean dishes cooked in a fire pit or a wood-fired oven, a focus on Canberra and Spanish wines, and a cozy dining room in a popular dining precinct

Buvette Bistro and Wine Bar

18 National Circuit, Barton 2600

Open: Breakfast 6.30 am to 10.30 am seven days, brunch
    11.30 am to 2.30 pm Sundays, lunch 12.00 pm to 3.00 pm
    Tuesday to Saturday, dinner 6.00 pm to 10.30 pm Tuesday to
    Saturday

Phone: 02 6163 1818

Website: **www.buvette.com.au**

Known for: French chic bistro and wine bar in a light, modern
    space in the Hotel Realm.

Capitol Bar and Grill

1 London Circuit, Canberra 2601

Open: Breakfast 6.30 am to 10.00 am (10.30 am weekends), then
    12.00 pm to 10.00 pm

Phone: 02 6247 1488

Website: **www.qthotelsandresorts.com/canberra/eat-drink/
    capitol-bar-grill**

Known for: Italian themed steaks, cocktails and a signature
    antipasto table in glamorous surroundings in the QT hotel.

Chairman and Yip

1 Burbury Close, Barton 2600

Open: Lunch 12.00 pm to 2.30 pm, dinner 6.00 pm to 10.30 pm
    Tuesday to Friday, 6.00 pm to 10.30 pm Saturday

Phone: 02 6162 1220

Website: **www.chairmangroup.com.au/chairmanyip**

Known for: Iconic Canberra institution serving high-end modern
    Cantonese cuisine in elegant surrounds in the Hotel Realm.

Courgette

54 Marcus Clarke Street, Canberra 2601

Open: Lunch 12.00 pm to 3.00 pm, dinner 6.00 pm to 11.00 pm
Monday to Saturday

Phone: 02 6247 4042

Website: **www.courgette.com.au**

Known for: Luxurious European fine dining and fine wines in a
plush dining room overlooking a walled garden.

Eightysix

20 Lonsdale St, Braddon 2612

Open: Breakfast 9 am till 11.30 weekends, lunch 12 pm till
2.30 pm weekends, dinner 6.00 pm till late Tuesday to Sunday

Phone: 02 6161 8686

Website: **www.eightysix.com.au**

Known for: Hipster, fun venue serving modern Australian share
plates in a bustling dining room with an open kitchen.

Italian and Sons

7 Lonsdale Street, Braddon 2612

Open: 12.00 pm to 2.00 pm and then 6.00 pm to 10.00 pm
Monday to Friday

6.00 pm to 9.00 pm Saturday Closed Sunday.

Phone: 02 6162 4888

Website: **www.italianandsons.com.au**

Known for: Popular upscale Italian trattoria with modern
interpretations of Italian classics Also check out the **Bacaro Wine
Bar** (page 148) in the same venue.

Lanterne Rooms

3/16 Blamey Place, Campbell 2612

Open: Lunch 12.00 pm to 2.30 pm Tuesday to Friday, dinner
6.00 pm to 10.00 pm Tuesday to Saturday

Phone: 02 6249 6889

Website: **www.chairmangroup.com.au/lanterne_rooms**

Known for: Owned by the same people as the acclaimed
Chairman & Yip. South-East Asian and Nyonya flavors in an
inviting, elegant space tucked away at the Campbell shops.

Lazy Su

1/9 Lonsdale Street, Braddon 2612

Open: Lunch Tuesday to Sunday and dinner seven days. Check the
website for details as times vary.

Phone: 02 5105 3812

Website: **www.lazy-su.com.au**

Known for: Casual, fun Korean/Japanese/American eating house
in hipster Braddon with retro decor and Asian-inspired cocktails
and sake.

Les Bistronomes

Corner of Elouera and Mort Street, Braddon 2601

Open: 12.00 pm to 2.00 pm and then 6.00 pm to 9.00 pm
Tuesday to Saturday

Closed Sunday.

Phone: 02 6248 8119

Website: **www.lesbistronomes.net**

Known for: A touch of Paris in Canberra with classic French cuisine
in a quaint bistro with fixed-price options, and an alfresco dining
area

Lilotang

Burbury Hotel, 1 Burbury Close, Barton 2600

Open: Lunch 12.00 pm to 2.30 pm Tuesday to Friday, dinner
6.00 pm to 11.00 pm Tuesday to Saturday

Phone: 02 6273 1424

Website: **www.chairmangroup.com.au/lilotang**

Known for: Fun, modern Japanese cuisine served in a slick
restaurant with blonde-wood paneling, cartoon details, bespoke
features and a sake list.

Mezzalira

55 London Circuit, Canberra 2601

Open: Lunch 12.00 pm to 2.30 pm Monday to Friday, dinner
6.00 pm to 10.00 pm Monday to Saturday

Phone: 02 6230 0025

Website: **www.mezzalira.com.au**

Known for: A longstanding Canberra favorite with a southern
Italian-inspired menu of handmade pasta, antipasti and fine
Italian and Australian wines.

Monster Kitchen and Bar

25 Edinburgh Avenue, Canberra 2601

Open: 6.30 am to 11.00 pm Monday to Friday and to 12.00 am
on weekends

Phone: 02 6287 6287

Website: **www.monsterkitchen.com.au**

Known for: Located in the lobby of the trendy Hotel Hotel in
NewActon precinct with diverse Modern Australian meals and
share plates focused on seasonal and local produce.

Kingston Foreshore Bars and Restaurants

Just east of the **Canberra Glassworks** (page 56) there's a small precinct dedicated to cafes, bars and restaurants on Eastlake Parade, near Trevillian Quay. From here you can base yourself for the day if you plan to hire a **GoBoat** (page 120) and take yourself on a do-it-yourself tour of Lake Burley Griffin.

It's also a good stopping point before or after a visit to the Sunday **Old Bus Depot Markets** (page 111). Here is the pick of the eateries along the Kingston Foreshore.

Molto

Element Building, 155/43 Eastlake Parade, Kingston 2604
Open: Lunch 12.00 pm to 3.00 pm Tuesday to Sunday, dinner
  6.00 pm to 10.00 pm seven days
Phone: 02 6140 7039
Website: **www.moltoitalian.com**
Known for: A modern Italian seaside trattoria with handmade
  pasta and woodfired pizza

Morks

18/19 Eastlake Parade, Kingston 2604
Open: Lunch 12.00 pm to 2.00 pm Wednesday to Friday and
  Sunday, dinner from 6.00 pm Tuesday to Sunday
Phone: 02 6295 0112
Website: **www.morks.com.au**
Known for: Inventive contemporary Thai dishes, sleek
  contemporary decor, a busy vibe and a 'secret' vegan menu. Not
  your usual Thai restaurant!

Tang Dynasty

10/81 Giles Street (near 33 Eastlake Parade), Kingston 2604

Open: Lunch 12.00 pm to 2.30 pm Monday and Wednesday to Friday, from 11.30 am weekends, dinner 6.00 pm to 9.30 pm every day except Tuesday

Phone: 02 6232 6997

Website: **www.tangdynasty.com.au**

Known for: Chinese fine dining and yum cha.

The Dock

7/81 Giles Street, Kingston 2604

Open: 11.30 am to 11.30 pm Tuesday to Saturday

Phone: 02 6239 6333

Website: **www.thedockkingston.com.au**

Known for: Live sports and entertainment and a menu of modern pub food offering something for everyone from fish and chips, burgers and pizzas to oysters and salads, with craft beers and local wines.

Walt & Burley

70/17 Eastlake Parade, Kingston 2604

Open: 11.00 am to 12.00 am seven days

Phone: 02 6239 6648

Website: **www.waltandburley.com.au**

Known for: Casual southern American style, pub classics and share plates in an expansive breezy space.

Natural Nine

21 Binara Street, Canberra 2608

Open: Lunch 12.00 pm to 2.30 pm, dinner 5.30 pm to 10.00 pm
  seven days

Phone: 02 6257 7074

Website: **www.natural9.com.au**

Known for: Well-regarded and reasonably priced Chinese-modern
  Australian fusion menu and yum cha in the Canberra Casino.
  Over 18s only.

Onred

50 Red Hill Drive, Red Hill 2603

Open: Lunch 12.00 pm to 3.00 pm Wednesday to Saturday, dinner
  from 5.30 pm Tuesday to Saturday

Phone: 02 6273 3517

Website: **www.onred.com.au**

Known for: One of the best views in Canberra with innovative
  seasonal dishes. The Coffee n Beans cafe is located on the
  ground floor if you're after a more casual food experience.

OTIS Dining Hall

29 Jardine Street, Kingston 2604

Open: Lunch 12.00 pm to 3.00 pm Tuesday to Saturday, dinner
  5.30 pm to 10.00 pm seven days

Phone: 02 6260 6066

Website: **www.thisisotis.com.au**

Known for: Clever modern takes on bistro classics and great
  cocktails in dark wood-paneled surroundings. Caters well for
  groups.

Ottoman

9 Broughton Street, Barton 2600

Open: Lunch 12.00 pm to 2.30 pm Tuesday to Friday, dinner
6.00 pm to 10.00 pm Tuesday to Saturday

Phone: 02 6273 6111

Website: **www.ottomancuisine.com.au**

Known for: Iconic Canberra restaurant serving up-market modern
Turkish meze and mains in a plush Art Deco room with views of
the gardens and water features.

Pilot

1 Wakefield Gardens, Ainslie 2612

Open: Lunch 12.00 pm to 3.30 pm Sunday, dinner 6.00 pm to late
Wednesday to Saturday

Phone: 02 6257 4334

Website: **www.pilotrestaurant.com**

Known for: Elegant, innovative high-end Australian cuisine with a
constantly changing menu.

Raku

148 Bunda Street, Canberra 2601

Open: Lunch 11.30 am to 3.00 pm, dinner 5.30 pm to 11.00 pm
seven days

Phone: 02 6248 6869

Website: **www.rakudining.com.au**

Known for: Sushi and grilled meat, seafood and vegetable dishes
that combine Japanese culinary traditions with the vibrant
energy of modern Australian dining.

Rubicon

6A Barker Street, Griffith 2603

Open: Lunch 12.00 pm to 2.30 pm Monday to Friday, dinner
6.00 pm to 10.30 pm Monday to Saturday

Phone: 02 6295 9919

Website: **www.rubiconrestaurant.com.au**

Known for: A welcoming atmosphere with a sophisticated modern
Australian menu served under fairy lights. Tucked away at the
Griffith shops, near **Aubergine** (page 129).

Sage Dining Rooms

Gorman House Arts Centre, Batman Street, Braddon 2612

Open: 12.00 pm to 11.00 pm Tuesday to Saturday

Phone: 02 6249 6050

Website: **www.sagerestaurant.net.au**

Known for: Modern Australian food in a1920s heritage building
with a comfortable dining room and the tranquil outdoor **Mint
Garden Bar** (page 150).

Temporada

15 Moore Street, Canberra 2601

Open: 7.30 am to 10.00 pm Monday to Friday, 5.00 pm till late
Saturday

Phone: 02 6249 6683

Website: **www.temporada.com.au**

Known for: Smart, modern eatery and bar serving produce-driven,
inventive tapas and share plates, an interesting wine list.

The Boathouse

Grevillea Park, Menindee Drive, Barton 2600

Open: Dinner from 6.30 pm Monday to Saturday

Phone: 02 6273 5500

Website: **www.theboathouse.restaurant**

Known for: Modern Australian dishes served in elegant lakeside surroundings with views across Lake Burley Griffin. A Canberra favorite for more than 20 years.

Vincent

48 Macquarie Street, Barton 2600

Open: Lunch 12.00 pm to 2 pm Wednesday to Friday, dinner 4.00 pm to 10.00 pm Tuesday to Saturday

Phone: 02 6273 7773

Website: **www.vincentrestaurant.com.au**

Known for: Fine dining paired with unconventional wines from around the world, a laid-back, moody atmosphere.

Water's Edge

Commonwealth Place, 40 Parkes Place, Parkes, 2600

Open: Lunch 12.00 pm to 3.00 pm, dinner 6.00 pm to 9.00 pm Wednesday to Sunday

Phone: 02 6273 5066

Website: **www.watersedgecanberra.com.au**

Known for: Modern Australian food in a lakeside dining room with white tablecloths and ceiling-high windows, right in the heart of the Parliamentary Triangle, on the edge of Lake Burley Griffin, as the name implies.

Bruncheries and Cafes

Although Canberra, like any city, has its fair share of cafes some are more noted than others, or at least have better marketing. Here is a selection to choose from, in particular ones that have a reputation for better food than the average cafe. Just make sure they're child-friendly if you plan on taking the wee ones.

Blue Olive Cafe

56 Alinga Street, Canberra 2601
Open: 7.00 am to 2.30 pm Monday to Friday
Phone: 02 6269 8815
Website: **www.blueolivecafe.com.au**
Known for: Sizable eats like burgers and New York style club sandwiches, in a buzzy location with sheltered outdoor tables.

Hyatt Hotel Canberra Tea Lounge Buffet

120 Commonwealth Avenue, Canberra 2600
Open: 2.30 pm to 5.00 pm weekends, first session from 11.00 am to 1.30 am Sunday
Phone: 02 6230 4600
Website: It's lengthy! Use your search engine.
Known for: The gorgeous and glamorous Art Deco Hyatt Hotel hosts an ever-popular weekend afternoon tea buffet with favorites including sandwiches, cakes, and scones with jam and cream. Bookings highly recommended and high tea stands are also available throughout the week.

Maple + Clove

Realm Park, 7 Burbury Close, Barton 2600

Open: 7.30 am to 3 pm Monday to Friday and 8.00 am to 3 pm
  weekends

Phone: 02 6162 0777

Website: **www.mapleandclove.com.au**

Known for: Sleek, airy cafe in leafy Barton focused on wholefoods,
  serving inventive brunch dishes and all-day breakfast on
  weekends.

Mocan and Green Grout

1/19 Marcus Clarke Street, Canberra 2601

Open: 7.00 am to 4.00 pm Monday, 7.00 am to 9.00 pm Tuesday
  to Saturday, 8.00 am to 2.00 pm Sunday

Phone: 02 6162 2909

Website: **www.mocanandgreengrout.com**

Known for: Located in the NewActon arts precinct, this hip, eco-
  friendly nook serves inventive meals cooked in an open kitchen,
  plus fair-trade espresso.

Morning Glory

NewActon Pavilion, 2/15 Edinburgh Avenue, Canberra 2601

Open: 7.00 am to 3.00 pm Sunday to Wednesday, 7.00 am to
  10.00 pm Thursday to Saturday

Phone: 02 6257 6464

Website: **www.morning-glory.com.au**

Known for: Minimalist interior and an interesting East meets West
  menu. Also opens for dinner three days a week.

Penny University Cafe

15 Kennedy Street, Kingston 2604

Open: 7.00 am to 3.30 pm seven days

Phone: 02 6162 1500

Website: **www.pennyuniversitycafe.com**

Known for: Funky, exposed-brick decor, great coffee and all-day breakfasts.

Ricardo's Cafe

Jamison Plaza, 1/1 Bowman Street, Macquarie 2614

Open: 7.30 am to 4.00 pm Saturday to Monday, 7.30 am to 5.30 pm Tuesday to Friday

Phone: 02 6251 2666

Website: **www.ricardoscafe.com**

Known for: The incredible creative and colorful Instagrammable cakes, pastries, and macarons with lots of gluten-free options. Very kid-friendly and convenient if you plan to visit the **Big Splash Waterpark** (page 101).

The Cupping Room

1/19 Marcus Clarke Street, Canberra 2601

Open: 7.00 am to 4.00 pm Monday to Friday, 8.00 am to 3.00 pm Wednesdays

Phone: 02 6257 6412

Website: **www.thecuppingroom.com.au**

Known for: Some of the best coffee in Canberra with the founder having been World Barista Champion in 2015. Busy and buzzy with specialty coffees and a menu of classic cafe staples.

Gastropubs

'Gastropub' is a word that combines the idea of gastronomy and pub. They're venues in which the eaties are as important as the drinkies – one up from a cafe but not quite fine dining. Nevertheless, the venues below are reputed to be wonderful places to eat and usually lend themselves to a relaxed, casual atmosphere.

Bar Rochford

65 London Circuit, Canberra 2601

Open: 5.00 pm to late Tuesday to Thursday, 3.00 pm to 1.00 am Friday 5.00 pm to 1.00 am Saturday

Phone: 02 6230 6222

Website: **www.barrochford.com**

Known for: Acclaimed wine and cocktail bar with well-regarded food at reasonable prices, a fireplace and music on a record player.

Debacle

Mode 3, 24 Lonsdale Street, Braddon 2612

Open: 11:30 am to late Monday to Friday,8:00 am to late weekends

Phone: 02 6247 1314

Website: **www.debacle.com.au**

Known for: Bustling, spacious family-friendly cafe/pub with pizza and upmarket pub dishes in an industrial-chic setting.

Ducks Nuts Bar & Grill

30 Woolley Street, Dickson 2602

Open: 11.00 am till late seven days

Phone: 02 6230 7675

Website: **www.ducksnuts.net.au**

Known for: Family-friendly sports bar and grill with an amazing range of beers, quality pub meals at reasonable prices and live music. It's near the **Dickson Aquatic Centre** (page 101) so you might want to eat here if you're having a sweltering day in Canberra.

Hopscotch

5 Lonsdale Street, Braddon 2612

Open: 11.00 am to 12.00 am seven days

Phone: 02 6107 3030

Website: **www.hopscotchbar.com.au**

Known for: Casual, fun atmosphere, quality pub grub (including an Argentine grill) and an extensive whiskey range, in a big, industrial-chic locale with a courtyard beer garden.

Public Bar

Manuka Arcade, 1–33 Flinders Way, Griffith 2603

Open: 10.00 am to late Monday to Friday, 9.00 am to late Saturday and Sunday

Phone: 02 6161 8808

Website: **www.public-bar.com.au**

Known for: Beautiful looking bar and restaurant for the beautiful people of **Manuka** with quirky share plates and up-market modern pub food, outdoor seating and great cocktails.

The Elk & Pea

3/21 Lonsdale Street, Braddon 2612

Open: 7.00 am to 11.00 pm Tuesday to Saturday, 7.00 am to 3.00 pm Sunday and Monday

Phone: 0436 355 732

Website: **www.elkandpea.com.au**

Known for: Creative food with a Latin American twist in an all-day eatery that's a hip cafe by day and bar by night, serving great cocktails in a vibrant, quirky space adorned with colourful paintings.

The Pedlar

65 Constitution Avenue, Campbell 2612

Open: 6.30 am to 11.00 pm seven days

Phone: 02 5100 5929

Website: **www.thepedlar.com.au**

Known for: If you're doing the walk around **Lake Burley Griffin** (page 118) and you're not even a quarter of the way and the weather, your mood, or your willpower suddenly goes bad then stroll up to The Pedlar and have something to eat or drink. With a varied menu of pub classic, burgers, salads and small plates, this fun family-friendly venue is not far from **Anzac Parade** (page 47) and the **Australian War Memorial** (page 44) either.

Historic Pubs

Enjoying Canberra can be dehydrating, so you'll want to sit down for a drink at some point. Some of these places are a little out of the way, but they give you an opportunity to explore the city beyond its center and maybe mix a little with the locals.

The Old Canberra Inn

195 Mouat Street, Lyneham 2602

Open: from 11.30 am to late seven days

Phone: 02 6134 6000

Website: **www.oldcanberrainn.com.au**

Known for: Atmosphere, historic architecture and live music, one of the earliest licensed pubs in the region. It's about 15 minutes' walk from the Dickson Light Rail stop.

The Rose Cottage Pub

Isabella Drive, Gilmore 2905

Open: Wednesdays from 3.00 pm till late, Thursday to Sunday from 10.00 am till late

Phone: 02 6260 1314

Website: **www.rosecottagecanberra.com**

Known for: Lovely outdoorsy setting and feel and bush country interior. They know they're on the outskirts so ask them about their courtesy bus to help you get there.

The Kingston Hotel

73 Canberra Avenue, Canberra 2603

Open: 10 am till late Monday to Saturday, 11 am till late Sunday

Phone: 02 6295 0123

Website: **www.kingstonhotel.com.au**

Known for: Being a popular family-friendly pub with live sports and well-priced food. If you know what you like you can even cook your own steak.

Traditional Pubs

The Civic Pub

8 Lonsdale Street, Braddon 2612

Open: 12.00 pm till late seven days

Phone: 02 6248 6488

Website: **www.civicpub.com.au**

Known for: Traditional bar decor and dining with a huge range of local and imported beers and a large pool room.

King O'Malley's

131 City Walk, Canberra 2601

Open: 11.00 am till late seven days

Phone: 02 6248 6488

Website: **www.kingomalleys.com.au**

Known for: Bistro meals in an old-time Irish tavern with a good selection of beers and whiskeys plus trivia, live music and a fire.

George Harcourt Inn

3 Gold Creek Road, Nicholls 2913

Open: 11.00 am till late seven days

Phone: 02 6248 6488

Website: **www.georgeharcourt.com**

Known for: Traditional English pub food, large outdoor area for warmer weather and a fire for the cold months, live music. It's also right in the heart of all the attractions at Gold Creek Village.

The Lighthouse Bar

80 Emu Bank, Belconnen 2913

Open: 11.00 am till late seven days

Phone: 02 6253 0390

Website: **www.lighthousepub.com.au**

Known for: Waterfront pub on Lake Ginninderra in Belconnen with live sports and music It's also near the **Canberra International Sports & Aquatic Centre** (page 102) and not too far from the **Australian Institute of Sport** (page 97).

The Durham Castle Arms

2 Jardine Street, Kingston 2604

Open: 12.00 pm till late seven days

Phone: 02 6295 1769

Website: **www.thedurhampub.com.au**

Known for: An English pub with cozy dark interiors, a wide range of craft beer on tap and well-priced pub food. It's also near the **Canberra Glassworks** (page 56) and **Old Bus Depot Markets** (page 111).

PJ O'Reilly's

52 Alinga Street, Canberra 2601

Open: 11.00 am till late Monday to Saturday

Phone: 02 6230 1261

Website: **www.pjoreillys.com.au**

Known for: Irish pub with casual dining, outdoor tables, trivia, live music and karaoke nights.

Bars

Those in the know are of the opinion that these are the best bars in Canberra, although some of them are hidden inside restaurants.

Bacaro Wine Bar

7 Lonsdale Street, Braddon 2612

Open: 5.30 pm till late Thursday to Saturday

Phone: 02 6162 4888

Website: **www.italianandsons.com.au/bacaro**

Known for: At the back of the **Italian and Sons** restaurant (page 131), stylish, sleek space with a fireplace and interesting bar food.

Highball Express

82 Alinga Street, Canberra 2601
Open: 4.00 pm till late Tuesday to Saturday
Phone: 02 6262 6522
Website: **www.highballexpress.com.au**
Known for: Cuban-themed tropical bar with a wide range of cocktails.

Hippo Co

1/17 Garema Place, Canberra 2601
Open: 5.00 pm till late Monday to Thursday and Saturday, 4.00 pm till late Friday
Phone: 02 6247 7555
Website: **www.hippoco.com.au**
Known for: Cocktail and jazz venue with a large collection of whiskeys.

Honkeytonks

17 Garema Place, Canberra 2601
Open: 3.00 pm till late Tuesday to Thursday, 12.00 pm till late Friday, 2.00 pm till late Saturday
Phone: 02 6262 6968
Website: **www.drinkhonkytonk.com.au**
Known for: Laid-back bar with a Tex-Mex theme specializing in cocktails and with craft beers on tap.

Joe's Bar at East Hotel

69 Canberra Avenue, Griffith 2603
Open: 4.00 pm till late Tuesday to Saturday
Phone: 02 6107 3030
Website: **www.easthotel.com.au/eat-and-drink/joes-bar**
Known for: Sophisticated small Italian-style wine bar with top-
notch food.

Knightsbridge Penthouse

1/34 Mort Street, Braddon 2612
Open: 5.00 pm till late Tuesday to Saturday
Phone: 02 6262 6221
Website: **www.knightsbridgepenthouse.com.au**
Known for: Hip lounge bar for cocktails with DJs playing soul, hip
hop and funk. Also has entertaining theme nights.

Lucky's Speakeasy

Ground Floor, QT Hotel, 1 London Circuit, Canberra 2601
Open: 6.00 pm till late Fridays and Saturdays
Phone: 02 6267 1200
Website: **www.qthotelsandresorts.com/canberra/eat-drink/
luckys-speakeasy**
Known for: Intimate, stylish bar with classic cocktails and bar
snacks and cool music.

Mint Garden Bar

Gorman House Arts Centre, Ainslie Avenue, Braddon 2601
Open: 3.00 pm till late Tuesday to Thursday, 12 pm till late Friday
and Saturday
Phone: 02 6249 6050

Website: **www.sagerestaurant.net.au/mint-garden-bar**

Known for: Tranquil bar with a lovely courtyard setting surrounded by heritage gardens, with cocktails, a lengthy wine list and interesting canapes and bar food.

Molly

Wooden Door, Odgers Lane, Canberra 2601

Open: 4.00 pm till late Monday to Saturday, 5 pm till late Sunday

Phone: 02 6179 8973

Website: **www.molly.bar**

Known for: Hidden behind an unassuming door, 1920s-style bar with great cocktails and live jazz.

Parlour

16 Kendall Lane, New Acton 2601

Open: 12.00 pm till late seven days

Phone: 02 6257 7325

Website: **www.parlour.net.au**

Known for: Tapas-style bar with Spanish share plates in an Art Deco room with plush furniture.

Playground

25 Garema Place, Canberra 2601

Open: 4.00 pm till late Thursday, Friday and Saturday

Phone: 02 6262 7171

Website: **www.playgroundbar.com.au**

Known for: Fun tapas and martini bar.

Polit Bar

Upstairs 8 Franklin Street, Manuka 2603
Open: Tuesday to Saturday 5.00 pm till late
Phone: 02 6162 2947
Website: **www.politbar.co**
Known for: Long-running, quirky hangout specializing in cocktails
with Italian-style pizza and comedy, live music and karaoke.

Smiths Alternative

76 Alinga Street, Canberra City 2601
Open: 12 pm till late seven days
Phone: 02 6257 1225
Website: **www.smithsalternative.com**
Known for: Formerly the much-loved Smiths Alternative Bookshop,
this arty cafe/bar hosts an eclectic range of performances from
comedy and improv theater to all types of live music.

Treehouse Bar

Sydney Building, 32 Northbourne Avenue, Canberra City 2601
Open: Wednesday 5.00 pm till late, Thursday and Friday 4.00 pm
till late, Saturday 6.00 pm till late
Phone: (02) 6162 0906
Website: **www.treehousebar.com.au**
Known for: Elegant bar with delicious tapas, burgers and cocktails
and live music.

Wineries

Considering that the Canberra region is dotted with wineries in beautiful surroundings it's almost as if you have a duty to visit them. The cool-climate wines from the Canberra region are highly acclaimed. Only a handful of the more than 140 vineyards and 30 cellar doors are located in the ACT with the rest over the border in New South Wales. Most are located around the town of Murrumbateman with another cluster on the other side of the city near Lake George. The main grape varieties of the Canberra region are riesling and shiraz but winemakers are increasingly planting other grape varieties suited to the climate and conditions.

If you have time for the drive to Murrumbateman or Lake George (each about 30 to 45 minutes from the city center) we recommend stopping at some of the cellar doors for a tasting. Here you can often chat to the winemaker as you sample a wine or two. We strongly suggest checking the website or phoning first to confirm that they can accommodate your visit on the day you want to travel. Many of these businesses are boutique and intimate and opening hours and days aren't always regular.

Among the more notable wineries are:

Brindabella Hills Winery

156 Woodgrove Close via Wallaroo Road, Hall, NSW 2618; Phone: 02 6188 5405; Website: **www.brindabellahills.com.au**; cellar door open for tastings and sales 10.00 am to 5.00 pm weekends and public holidays and for sales only on weekdays.

Clonakilla

3 Crisps Lane (off Murrumbateman Road), Murrumbateman,
NSW 2582, Phone: 02 6227 5877; Website: **www.clonakilla.com.au**;
cellar door open 11.00 am to 4.00 pm weekdays, 10.00 am to
5.00 pm weekends.

Collector Wines

7 Murray Street, Collector, NSW 2581; Phone: 0415 991 078;
Website: **www.collectorwines.com.au**; cellar door open 10.00 am
to 4.00 pm Thursday to Sunday.

Helm Wines

19 Butts Road, Murrumbateman, NSW 2582; Phone:
02 6227 5953; Website: **www.helmwines.com.au**; cellar door open
Thursday to Sunday from 10.00 am to 4.00 pm in winter and
10.00 am to 5.00 pm in summer.

Lake George Winery

Federal Highway, Lake George, NSW 2581; Phone: 02 4848 0182;
Website: **www.lakegeorgewinery.com.au**; cellar door open
10.00 am to 5.00 pm Thursday to Sunday.

Lark Hill

521 Bungendore Road (corner of Bungendore Road and Joe Rocks
Road), Bungendore, NSW 2621; Phone: 02 6238 1393; Website:
www.larkhillwine.com; cellar door open 11.00 am to 4.00 pm
Wednesday to Monday.

Lerida Estate

87 The Vineyards, Federal Highway, Lake George, NSW 2581;
Phone: 02 4848 0231; Website: **www.leridaestate.com.au**;
cellar door open 10.00 am to 5.00 pm daily.

Mount Majura Vineyard

88 Lime Kiln Road, Majura 2609; Phone: 02 6262 3070; Website:
mountmajura.com.au; cellar door open 10.00 am to 5.00 pm daily.

Pialligo Estate Canberra

18 Kallaroo Road, Pialligo 2609; Phone: 02 6247 6060; Website:
thepialligoestate.com.au; cellar door open by appointment only;
restaurant open Wednesday to Sunday.

Poachers Pantry Smokehouse Restaurant & Wiley Trout Vineyard

431 Nanima Road, Springrange, NSW 2618; Phone: 02 6230 2487;
Website: **www.poacherspantry.com.au**; cellar door open 9.30 am
to 5.00 pm daily.

Shaw Wines

34 Isabel Drive, Murrumbateman, NSW 2582; Phone:
02 6227 5827; Website: **www.shawwines.com.au**; cellar door
open 10.00 am to 5.00 pm daily.

Breweries

If you prefer grain to grapes then these may tempt you.

Bentspoke Brewing Company

38 Mort Street Braddon 2612, (entry from Elouera Street); Phone: 02 6257 5220; Website: **www.bentspokebrewing.com.au**; open 11.00 am to 12.00 am daily.

Big River Distilling Company

Tenancy 3, Building 3, 1 Dairy Road, Fyshwick 2609; Phone: 0490 038 457; Website: **www.bigriverdistilling.com.au**; open 12.00 pm to 6.00 pm Friday to Sunday, 12.00 pm to 5.00 pm Wednesday and Thursday.

Capital Brewing Co

Building 3, 1 Dairy Road, Fyshwick 2609; Phone: 02 5104 0915; Website: **www.capitalbrewing.co**; open 11.30 am to 3.00 pm Monday to Thursday and Sunday, 11.30 am to late Friday and Saturday; tours available and the original red **Brodburger** caravan is located on site for meals. Kids and dogs welcome.

Zierholz Premium Brewery

Unit 7/19–25 Kembla Street, Fyshwick 2609; Phone: 02 5105 3664; Website: **www.zierholz.com.au**; open 11.30 am till late Friday, 11.30 am to 3.30 pm Wednesday, Thursday and Saturday.

Wine and Brewery Tours

Perhaps the best way to visit a winery if you don't have your own transport is to go on a wine or brewery tour. Even if you have a car, let someone else do the driving so you can relax and sample the wares.

Canberra Guided Tours

Phone: 0408 483 770
Website: **www.canberraguidedtours.com.au/tours/cool-climate-wine-experience**
All-day tours cost $149 per person and visit between four and six wineries for tastings.

Canberra Winery Tours

Phone: 02 6299 9898
Website: **www.canberrawinerytours.com**
Tours include but not limited to Silver Package (3 stops from $200 per person) and Gold Package (5 stops from $250 per person).

Dave's Brewery Tours

Phone: 02 9318 0853
Website: **www.daves.com.au/canberra**
Tours include but are not limited to Capital 3 in 3 (from $130 per person) and Capital Highlander Tour (from $190 per person).

Vines & Wines

Phone: 0432 807 316
Website: **www.vineswines.com.au**
Minibus tour run every second Saturday visiting four wineries and stopping for lunch, $175 per person. Check the website for details of upcoming tours. Private tours are also available.

First published in 2019 by New Holland Publishers
London • Sydney • Auckland

Bentinck House, 3–8 Bolsover Street, London W1W 6AB, UK
1/66 Gibbes Street, Chatswood, NSW 2067, Australia
5/39 Woodside Ave, Northcote, Auckland 0627, New Zealand

newhollandpublishers.com

A record of this book is held at the British Library and the National
Library of Australia.

ISBN 9781760791339

Group Managing Director: Fiona Schultz
Author: Xavier Waterkeyn
Project Editor: Liz Hardy
Designer: Andrew Davies
Production Director: Arlene Gippert
Printer: Toppan Leefung Printing Limited

10 9 8 7 6 5 4 3 2 1

Keep up with New Holland Publishers:
NewHollandPublishers
@newhollandpublishers

Picture credits: All images are from Shutterstock except: Bidgee (page 54);
Coordinate123 (page 110); CSIRO (page 81); Grahamec (page 58); Walter Burley
Griffin (page 14); Maksym Kozlenko (page 83); Stuart Lindenmayer (page 60);
Nick-D (page 57, 104, 111)